To Ralph Hufford
With best wishes

Findley B. Edge

Bought used - RLM

A Quest for Vitality in Religion

A
QUEST FOR
VITALITY IN RELIGION

A Theological Approach
to Religious Education

Findley B. Edge

BROADMAN PRESS *Nashville, Tennessee*

Library of Congress catalog card number: 63—8406

Printed in the United States of America

3.5O6313

To

Larry and Hoyt

Contents

PART II

The Nature and Meaning of the Christian Life

PART III

How One Enters the Christian Life

PART IV
Seeking a Regenerate Church Membership

Preface

At the present time churches are experiencing a period of almost unparalleled popularity and prosperity. Such a situation normally would be the basis for unrestrained optimism and rejoicing. Strangely, such is not the case. Many thoughtful religious leaders and mature Christian laymen evidence a growing ferment of uneasiness and concern. In spite of plush church buildings, growing membership, and many vigorous activities that are carried on within the churches, something is seriously wrong with modern Christianity. Something is wrong at its center. It is in danger of losing its life and dynamic. "The Church is like a ship on whose deck festivities are still kept up and glorious music is heard, while deep below the water-line a leak has been sprung and masses of water are pouring in, so that the vessel is settling hourly lower though the pumps are manned day and night."[1] If this is true, our problem is no minor matter. For those of us who have given our lives to God, this strikes at the very center of our existence. We do not want to let the church die in our hands, nor by our failure do we want to contribute to its failure. Therefore, this book is written as a call to those who are concerned.

A basic thesis of this work is that many evidences indicate that institutionalism is threatening the vitality of our churches. No wonder the concerned person feels frustrated when he ponders what can be done to change the situation. He faces a

---

[1] Karl Heim, *Christian Faith and Nutural Science* (New York: Harper & Bros., 1953, p. 24.

formidable task. Many ask: Can we stem this tide toward institutionalism and recapture experiential religion? The question cannot be answered easily or conclusively. History indicates that all movements tend to become institutionalized. This is what happened to the religious movements of the past, and the modern religion movement will be no exception. The "determinist" in sociology claims that the pattern of this sociological phenomenon is inevitable. It cannot be changed. Others, however, believe that human beings can exercise "purposive control" and thus to some extent shape and direct the movement of which we are a part. Whether we will be sufficiently intelligent and courageous to exercise this purposive control only the future will tell.

The solution will call for radical and daring action on the part of Christian leaders and church members. It will be necessary to clarify afresh what we as the "people of God" are to be and do in the modern world in the light of the teachings of the Scriptures. To identify some of the major doctrines involved and to indicate what the life and work of the church must be in the light of these doctrines is the major task of this book. A theological position is assumed. Little effort is made to defend the position taken. Rather, the main purpose here is to ask: Given this theological position, what should the church be and do in light of these doctrines?

Chapter 1 seeks to point up the problem which is the burden of the entire book. Religion seems to be thriving in our day. But what kind of religion is it? Is it really the faith of the New Testament, or have we unconsciously wandered far from it? Some admit that there are weaknesses in the church today, but they insist that these are only minor maladies which are always with us. How can we tell whether our current weaknesses are merely minor maladies or whether they are more serious in nature? By what standard can we ascertain whether apparent success is the real thing?

It is only against the backdrop of the New Testament and Christian history that these questions can be answered. Part I seeks to provide this backdrop by giving a survey of three religious movements, each of which began as a vital, dynamic movement, became highly successful, but then lapsed into a cold and lifeless formalism as its expression of religion. In these religious movements of the past, we can see our own immediate past reflected; we can identify our present; and with some imagination we might be able to forecast our future. Against this backdrop of history, we seek to analyze our present situation.

Part II begins the analysis of the present situation in our churches with an inquiry into the nature and meaning of the Christian life. When God calls a person to be Christian, what does he call him to be and do? This question is explored in light of the doctrine of election, the doctrine of the priesthood of believers, and the concept of the will of God.

With the answers given in Part II as a background, Part III then considers the question: How does one enter the Christian life? Here the doctrine of man is examined to ascertain man's basic need and also to discover what God has done to meet man in his need. In the light of the answers found a suggestion is made as to what one of the basic tasks of the church must be. Following this the exceedingly difficult question is faced: If man is saved "by grace through faith," what is involved in "faith"? There is an authentic faith that is fundamental in the saving relationship, yet there is also a spurious faith which, according to the book of James, is worthless. What is the nature of this authentic faith? In light of the answers given, suggestions are made as to the approach to evangelism that should be followed by the church.

Finally in Part IV the question is asked: How can we more adequately approach the ideal of a regenerate church membership? Although we make the claim of practicing "believer's baptism" only, most will admit that in reality we do not now have a regenerate church membership. Should we seek to find better ways of implementing this doctrine or should we continue to compromise? If we undertake seriously to implement this doctrine, what must be done in the life and work of the church?

One of the most difficult decisions that had to be made concerned the audience to whom the book should be addressed. Should it be addressed to the larger Christian fellowship or specifically to my own denomination? The first and natural inclination was to write to the larger Christian community. It is my belief that the problem with which this work is concerned is probably the basic problem of all communions. Also it is only natural for one who writes to desire to have as large a potential audience as possible.

The decision was made, however, to relate the book to my own denomination for the following reasons: First, to address the book to the larger fellowship would have necessitated writing it in far more general terms, but in so doing it would have lost the "cutting edge" of being specific, which the nature of the problem desperately demands. Second, I was not sufficiently familiar with the inner workings of other denominations, and lacking this specific information, I was not competent to analyze the life and program of their churches. Third, an analysis of this type, which at times may be critical, should be undertaken by one who is an insider, one who positively identifies himself with his group, who rejoices in the successes that are genuine and willingly accepts his share of the responsibility for the weaknesses. Fourth, it seemed that making a specific approach to one denomination would be best even for readers of other communions. That is, where I have undertaken to be specific in pointing to weaknesses in the work of my denomination, the reader would be stimulated to consider whether this or a similar weakness exists in his denomination. Where I have made specific proposals for my denomination, the reader would evaluate the proposal in terms of the life and work of his religious group—at least such is the hope.

Some will say that the proposals suggested herein are radical and unrealistic. To say that they are radical does not say that they are wrong. To say that they are unrealistic may simply

be an indication of how far down the road toward institutionalism the modern church has traveled. One question has dominated my thinking in this study: In the light of the teachings
of the Scriptures what ought we as the people of God to be in
the modern world? To discover what this means and recapture
its essence in the life and work of the church is our basic task—
regardless of how drastic the changes that may be involved. The
patterns of the past, the traditions of men, or the cry "let's be
practical" must not thwart this fundamental quest.

Others may feel that the position taken and the solutions
suggested are merely the idealistic musings of a professor in
an "ivory tower" wholly unrelated to the real problems and
needs in the "front lines" of our churches. This is partly true
and, I hope, partly false. As a teacher of religious education, I
have had considerable contact with the problems and needs of
churches as well as with life as it is lived in our churches. On
the other hand, my major ministry has not been in the churches
themselves. In one sense, much of my ministry may be said to
have been spent in a "tower," but this is not a bad vantage point
from which to view our religious situation. Often the one on the
"front lines" is so concerned with the immediate needs that he
is unable to see the whole battle in its long-range perspective.
On the "front lines" one is tempted to make decisions and take
courses of action based on the immediate pressures of the mo-
ment without adequate recognition of their long-range consequences. In such instances, one is tempted to confuse things
as they are with things as they ought to be. Thus, a view from
a "tower" does have its place and may make a significant contribution.

Some also may wonder why I, whose work is in religious
education, have undertaken to grapple with these difficult theological problems. The answer is quite simple. While I as a
religious educator am concerned with the forms, programs, and
techniques through which the gospel is communicated, I want
to make sure that it is the *true gospel* that is being communicated through these means. For this reason the person in

religious education must always be deeply concerned about theology.

I acknowledge my indebtedness to those students who have explored these areas with me in seminars. By their incisive questions and their keen insights they often became my teachers. Several friends read the first draft and, besides giving constructive criticisms, encouraged me to continue the work. Among these were Ernest J. Loessner, Robert A. Proctor, C. Penrose St. Amant, J. Leo Garrett, and W. W. Adams, all on the faculty of the Southern Baptist Theological Seminary; Kenneth L. Chafin, Southwestern Baptist Theological Seminary; Brooks Ramsey, First Baptist Church, Albany, Georgia; Ellis Bush, Baptist Sunday School Board; Randolph C. Miller, Yale University Divinity School; G. Campbell Wyckoff, Princeton Theological Seminary; and Donald M. Maynard, Boston University School of Theology. To all of these I express my genuine appreciation. Two colleagues deserve a special word: Allen W. Graves and William E. Hull read the final manuscript and made numerous and helpful suggestions. For their assistance I am deeply grateful. Badgett Dillard and Clara McCartt rendered valuable assistance in matters of style, and Mrs. Glenn Hinson typed the final manuscript. To them, my thanks. Finally, I express appreciation to my wife, Louvenia Littleton Edge, and to my two sons, Larry and Hoyt, who share with me both the concern and the hope expressed in this book.

FINDLEY B. EDGE

Louisville, Kentucky

1

Experiential or Institutionalized Religion?

Two paradoxical phenomena may be seen in the religious life of the United States today. On the one hand are numerous evidences that religion is in the midst of a period of unparalleled success. On the other, a crescendo of voices, raised both in question and warning, point up the fact that something is seriously wrong with modern Christianity.

Which of these conflicting views is correct? Is it possible that there is a real measure of accuracy in both views? If so, which view is more critical and, therefore, demands our primary concern?

Evidences of Revival

It is obvious that there has been a revival of religion in this generation. Church membership has reached an all-time high. In 1850 only 16 per cent of the population were members of any church. During the next fifty years, by 1900, this had risen to 36 per cent. In 1940 church membership was 49 per cent, while in 1960 it had risen to 63.4 per cent. In the two decades between 1920 and 1940 church membership increased only 6 per cent; while in the two decades between 1940 and 1960 it increased 14.4 per cent. In 1943 (more adequate statistics are given for this year than in 1940) there were approximately 213,000 Sunday schools with an enrolment of just over 25,000,000. In 1960 there were over 286,000 Sunday schools with an enrolment of over 44,000,000.[1] This is an increase of a million

[1] *Yearbook of American Churches for 1961* (New York: National Council of the Churches of Christ in the U.S.A., 1960), pp. 264, 279.

per year in enrolment for nearly twenty years—a remarkable growth.

Attendance at the services in the churches has likewise increased. "Opinion polls of attendance at church by adults indicated that 41 per cent of the respondents attended in the week preceding the interview in 1939 as compared to 51 per cent in 1957." [2] One of the most remarkable areas of growth has been that of finances. Between 1940 and 1960 contributions to churches more than doubled. In 1940 total gifts of more than $1,100,000,000, were reported. In 1960 total gifts were a little over $2,300,000,000. In 1950 the per capita giving was $30.51. In 1960 it was $62.25. Despite inflation this is a significant gain.

Church construction has soared to new heights. New churches are being built; old churches are being remodeled, or new space is being added. It is true that building is directly related to the economy, and we have had prosperous years recently. Yet in comparing the present building surge with another prosperous year, 1928, we find there is approximately a 400 per cent increase at the present time. Church building has become "the fourth largest private building category" as religious bodies have "erected tangible symbols of their devotion."[3]

Statistics alone cannot measure the depth of religious concern, nor are these the only evidences of success that might be cited. However, they do give an indication of the progress being made and the interest and attention currently given to religion by a majority of our population.

What Kind of Religion Is It?

Many evidences thus point to the fact that for the past two decades in particular there has been a rather remarkable renaissance in religion. Some call it a "revival of religion"; some, an "interest in religion"; others refer to it as a "surge of piety." However it may be characterized, it cannot be denied that

---

[2] Gibson Winter, *The Suburban Captivity of the Churches* (Garden City, N. Y.: Doubleday & Co., Inc., 1961), p. 30.

[3] Martin E. Marty, *The New Shape of American Religion* (New York: Harper & Bros., 1959), p. 15.

there has been a definite "upswing" in religion. Although the forward progress has slowed to some extent recently, the optimism of many concerning the future of religion in the United States is undiminished.

The question being raised with increasing frequency and with growing concern, however, is: What kind of religious revival are we experiencing in our generation? Is it in reality a revival of the Christian faith, the faith of the New Testament, or is it something other than the Christian faith? Have we developed a religion that holds to the external forms of the New Testament faith but places something else at the center?

In answer to this question Claire Cox says,

There is a new-time religion in the land. It has made the church more popular and prosperous than ever before. It also has made the church less pious. . . . What this religious phenomenon is no one is exactly sure. Many a churchman has spent painful hours pondering the question. There is no doubt about the heightened religious interest. . . . But the religious upsurge appears against a dismal backdrop of payola, television quiz show "fixes," police scandals, increasing rape, murder, robbery and embezzlement, and rising rates of juvenile delinquency, alcoholism and divorce.[4]

Roy Eckardt calls the religion which is having such a resurgence in America today "folk religion."

The real justification of the phrase "folk religion" is the fact that the "turn to religion" is very much a popular movement. . . . Folk religion is religion for the "folks." It is characterized by the fact that it holds both the people and religion in high esteem. . . . Piety can resolve basic human problems of both a personal and social nature, and this without very great difficulty. Religion is marked by its utility.[5]

Others suggest that instead of the religion of the New Testament, in reality we have developed a "new American religion" which tends to be identified with the highest ethical standards

[4] *The New-Time Religion* (Englewood Cliffs, N. J.: Prentice-Hall, Inc., 1961), pp. 1-2.
[5] *The Surge of Piety in America* (New York: Association Press, 1958), p. 43.

of modern society. The interest in and commitment to this "new American religion" is very deep and very real. The only difficulty is that this is not the New Testament faith. Will Herberg, in his penetrating analysis of modern religion, says that today we have a sort of "religion in general" that affirms the "American way of life." Church members are more deeply committed to the American way than they are to "the way" of the first century. In fact they seem to have identified the American way and "the way" as being synonymous. When probed deeply, the average American is more concerned about and opposed to one who threatens the American way of life than to one who might threaten his religion.[6]

The warning being raised is that this "new American religion" has lost much of the essence and vitality that was characteristic of New Testament Christianity. Marty describes the change that has taken place in this fashion:

From the days when reformed Christians came to America . . . to the present, Protestantism has carried on an exciting dialogue with its environment. The characteristic result we have described as *erosion*. Constant friction rubbed rough edges away. Protestant particularity and the offense of its witness tended to be worn smooth; uncongenial aspects in the American environment were absorbed. Church (or churches) and world made their peace. Religion was Americanized and America was religionized, and both were accepted complacently.[7]

It should not be inferred from what has been said or will be said that there are not those people in our churches who have a genuine personal faith and a deep commitment to Jesus Christ. Unfortunately, these are the exception and not the rule. The average member of our churches neither reflects an intelligent awareness of the deeper demands of the Christian faith as a radical way of life, nor does he demonstrate a serious commitment of himself to that way of life.

Certainly the typical church member believes in God. In fact

---

[6] *Protestant, Catholic, Jew* (Garden City, N. Y.: Doubleday & Co., Inc., 1955), pp. 89-90.

[7] *Op. cit.,* p. 108.

polls indicate that over 90 per cent of our total population attest to their belief in God. But what kind of God is it in which the typical member believes? Is he the God of Abraham, Isaac, and Jacob? Is he the one so holy and majestic that mortal man bows in his presence in reverence and awe? No, this is not the temper of our times. Americans have not only come to "know" God, they have become "chummy" with him. To one he is a "living doll"; to another he is the "man upstairs." We are on his side and he is on our side. This God "smiles on society, and his message is a relaxing one. He does not scold you; he does not demand of you. He is a gregarious God and he can be found in the smiling, happy people of the society about you. As the advertisement puts it, religion can be fun." [8]

Certain leading psychiatrists are writing today that belief in God is essential for a sound, integrated personality. Politicians are proclaiming that only a return to God can preserve our way of life. Scientists are saying that a spiritual transformation is essential if our civilization is to survive. So, in our generation, there has been a "turning to God," a return to religion.

This modern infatuation with religion was typified in a recent cartoon. A man was pictured in clerical garb. On his lapel was a large (campaign-size) button with the words: "I Like God." God would get his vote. In fact God would get the vote of the majority of Americans. They "like God." Yet this "belief in God" does not seriously affect the minor or major relationships of most people. Although the overwhelming majority professes to a belief in God, "three out of four admit they never think of God in relation to their own lives or associate Him with their behavior."[9] When there is a conflict between the ways of God and current social mores, the latter is almost always the course that is followed.

What we have failed to understand is that our return has

[8] William H. Whyte, Jr., *The Organization Man* (New York: Simon and Schuster, 1956), p. 254.
[9] Ardis Whitman, "What Not to Tell a Child About God," *Reader's Digest*, February, 1962, pp. 81-82.

been to "religion" and not to Christianity; our revival has been a "religious" revival and not, primarily, a revival of Christianity. What the typical church member does not understand is that God does not exist to give us peace of mind, to save our way of life, nor even to save our civilization. As Perry says, "the God of Christian faith is no bell-hop catering to our needs as we define them and to our vanities and aspirations. We are God's servants, citizen-subjects of his kingdom, performing his service when he beckons." [10] When God demands of his people a radical break with the evils and injustices of modern society, when he demands a radical break with the "cult of conformity" that has engulfed modern religion, the one who would be Christian rather than merely religious has no choice but to obey. We must serve God. God does not exist to serve us.

Although it is true that a majority of present-day Americans are members of some church, this does not mean that they have given themselves to God to do his will "on earth even as it is done in heaven." The fact is that the labor union, the manufacturers' association, or the professional society of which they are members exerts far more influence on their attitudes, values, and courses of action. These relationships demand and get more real loyalty from the average man than does the church to which he belongs.

Modern society expects the church to make a comfortable adjustment to current social norms, and the church usually has been ready to comply. The distinction between church and world, between the people of God and the people of the world, has largely been lost. The masses join the churches with a minimum of commitment and with a minimum being expected of them.

Success-minded congregations make it all too clear in their solicitation that admission to the church is by handshake with the smiling pastor. The church that opens its door so easily loses its potency. . . . Few are asked to take the form of a servant, but all are frequently

[10] Edmund Perry, *The Gospel in Dispute* (Garden City, N. Y.: Doubleday & Co., Inc., 1958), p. 16.

asked to take a packet of envelopes for financial contributions. No one is religious because everyone is "religious."[11]

How is it that such a situation exists in the life of churches today? Undoubtedly there are numerous reasons. For example, many people have united with a church for other than Christian reasons. Some have joined for purely business reasons rather than on the basis of a personal commitment to Jesus Christ. The public schoolteacher knows that she will be more readily accepted by the community if she joins the church. The insurance man knows it is good business if he is active in the life of a church. In *Sincerely, Willis Wayde,* a novel by John P. Marquand, the hero, an up-and-coming young executive, moves to a new community, joins the church, and becomes a solicitor for the every-member canvass.

Willis Wayde is a complete secularist without the vaguest glimmering of what the Christian religion is all about. But he knows that the up-and-coming young executive, moving into a suburban community of other up-and-coming young executives, is expected to be identified with a Protestant church.[12]

Also, in belonging to a church an individual may be fulfilling no more than a basic desire of modern man, the desire to belong, to be identified with and accepted by his fellow man. It is true that he may have a vague admiration for an Isaiah, an Elijah, or an Amos, but he has no real identification with these "zealots for the Lord." To exhibit such nonconformity, to hold such an uncompromising position before his fellow man would be impossible for him. His need for belonging, his need to be accepted is too great. The religion of the modern man

is thus frequently a religiousness without serious commitment, without real inner conviction, without genuine existential decision. What should reach down to the core of existence, shattering and renewing, merely skims the surface of life, and yet succeeds in generating

[11] Marty, *op. cit.,* p. 117.
[12] Paul Hutchinson, *The New Ordeal of Christianity* (New York: Association Press, 1957), p. 113.

the sincere feeling of being religious. Religion thus becomes a kind of protection the self throws up against the radical demand of faith.[13]

Is Christianity Becoming Institutionalized?

The thoughtful observer views contemporary religion with mixed emotions. He may be raised to the heights of rejoicing as he views the many evidences of success, of genuine concern for the unreached and unsaved, of unselfish dedication and service on the part of many. On the other hand, he may be plunged almost to the depths of despair, for the thoughtful observer cannot help but be aware that there are also disturbing evidences of tendencies toward externalism, superficiality, and institutionalism in modern religious life.

There is always good and bad, strength and weakness, in the expression of religion at any given time. Weakness may show up even when the church is at its best, and some strength is there when the church is at its worst. This analysis of the current religious situation does not mean to imply that our understanding, appropriation, and expression of religion today has been a complete failure. The question is whether, through the passing years, we have unconsciously wandered from and thus tended to lose the essential spirit and vitality of the faith of the New Testament, so that today we merely are holding on to some of the external forms of that faith.

In assessing the modern religious situation, some people emphasize the other side of the picture. "What is wrong," they ask, "with religion becoming a vogue in American life? . . . Let's be glad for the faithful fifties. If this generation will move with the winds of God as we now see them stirring in our American life, we may see one of the most memorable acts of God in the history of mankind." [14] If one feels that the religion of today is the religion of the New Testament, or a reasonable facsimile thereof, then one will agree with the previous statement. Those holding this view will feel that a book such as

---

[13] Herberg, *op. cit.*, p. 276.
[14] Quoted in Eckhardt, *op. cit.*, p. 158.

this is out of place and does more damage than good. They feel we need to stop criticizing, stop "rocking the boat." They feel we need to get together to promote and expand the religion of today with every ounce of energy that is within us.

On the other hand, if religion as it is being expressed today, in the main, is not the religion of the New Testament and only in certain external forms is it even a partial facsimile thereof, then to perpetuate the current religious expression is to bring upon us the judgment of God. Thus, one's reaction to the current religious situation is determined by one's answer to the question: What is the nature and essence of New Testament religion? To explore this question and to suggest a possible answer is one purpose of this study.

First we must consider what is meant by "institutionalism" in religion. It is no broadside condemnation of institutions and organizations *per se*. They are both necessary and desirable instruments for the orderly and adequate propagation of the faith. They provide an effective means by which converts to the movement are made. They provide the structure in which and through which guidance is given to the adherents through teaching and study. They provide an effective means of cooperation by which the adherents as a group can accomplish tasks which are too large and complicated for individuals to do alone. Thus, it would be utterly impossible for any movement to survive without institutions and organizational structure. Certainly it would be impossible for any adequate propagation of the values of the movement to be made without such institutions. Institutions are not inherently evil. Rather they are a valid and valuable part of any significant movement.

What, then, is meant by "institutionalism"? Religion becomes institutionalized when its adherents are related primarily to the church as an institution or to the organizations of the church rather than to the living God. The religious life manifested is not the free and open outworking of a deep, spiritual relationship with God. Rather, in institutionalized religion the primary expression of a person's religion is that he supports the organizations by his attendance; he supports the institution by his gifts; and in general he merely lives a "good" life.

Acknowledging this as a real trend today would depend, in part, upon the religious group or groups with which one has had contact and also, in part, upon the criteria used in making one's evaluation. To be precise in such a subjective matter is virtually impossible. It is the conclusion of one writer, however, that

approximately one half of the official membership of the churches, possibly as much as two thirds, are religiously tied to an organization rather than personally bound to God or his teachings—a surprising fact in view of the Protestant understanding of faith. It is ironical that Protestantism, after rebelling against the institutional character of Roman Catholicism, should emerge in the 1960s with a membership predominantly oriented to organizational activities.[15]

Religion becomes institutionalized when the church turns its concern inward upon itself, when it is more concerned with its own existence and progress than it is with the mission for which it was founded. Hendrik Kraemer says this is exactly what is happening in the modern church.

. . . The Church as such is introvert, and considered as such by public opinion. It has been bred for centuries into the Church and therefore it is felt as natural by Church people themselves and by public opinion . . . the mind of the Churches is bent, above all, on its own increase and well-being. It is Church-centred. It is self-centred.[16]

It is true that Protestants have demonstrated an interest in and concern for the unreached masses. We have taken a definite pride in the fact that our Sunday school enrolment has increased twenty million in less than twenty years. The increase in church membership likewise has been a source of pride. But this very outreach, which indeed is a fundamental part of the Christian mission in the world, too often seems only to have contributed to the growth of the church as an *institution*. The churches

---

[15] Winter, *op. cit.*, p. 100.
[16] *A Theology of the Laity* (London: Lutterworth Press, 1958), p. 127.

have not seriously attempted to transform the world, nor have we led the people whom we have reached and enlisted to be active instruments in remaking the world.

One primary motive that underlies the multitudinous activities carried on by the minister and the people is to build up and enlarge the institution. In their minds this has come to be identified with "doing the will of God." The truth of this statement is demonstrated by noting the question which ministers and other staff members generally ask each other: What's your Sunday school enrolment now? How many baptisms did you have last year? What's your church budget? "The church-as-an-institution is more concerned to enhance the institution than it is to minister to the real needs of people or to transform the world. In such a situation, the office of the minister becomes the job of a promoter."[17]

Religion becomes institutionalized when means become ends and ends become means. Institutions and organizations which were designed and intended to be used as a means of serving people may become ends, and the loyalty of people is determined by their service to the institution.

We have reached a time when conventional American Protestant churches are inordinately concerned with upholding the existence, the authority, and the sanctity of their own organizational structures. Forms of organization which originated as *means* to enable the church to function "decently and in order" in performing its redemptive mission, have become ends to be served. . . . Instead of using organizations to serve people, we use people to serve organizations. . . . This is fatal. The church which seeks to save its own life will lose it, just as surely as the person who seeks to save his life will lose it.[18]

The announcements made in church about certain meetings are indicative of the emphasis on organizational ends. For example, we often hear the Sunday school superintendent announcing: "The regular Sunday school associational meeting will be held

---

[17] John W. Meister, "Requirements for Renewal," *Union Seminary Quarterly Review*, XVI, March, 1961, p. 254-255.
[18] *Ibid.*, pp. 253-254.

this afternoon at Red Fork Church. Brother Smith is our new associational superintendent and he is trying real hard to have a good attendance. Let's all try to be present and support him in his work." Or: "We're having the associational Training Union meeting in our church this afternoon. It would be embarrassing if some other church should have more in attendance than we do. Let's all try to come."

Support the organization. This is the emphasis! Attend the meeting. This is how to demonstrate your loyalty! Little or nothing is said about the real purpose of the meeting or about what the meeting is to do for those who attend. Of course there is a vague idea that those who attend "might be helped." But if the attendance of the organizations goes down, it is the task of the leadership of the church to increase this attendance. The loyalty and devotion of the church members are largely determined by their faithful attendance at the meetings of the church. What they do or do not do for Christ *in the world* is not the central concern. The organizations must be served!

Religion becomes institutionalized when it is more concerned with the correctness of one's belief than it is with the quality of one's life. Institutions are founded to propagate values that are held in highest esteem by a group. In the beginning of a movement the life of the group is directed by and lived under the demand of these values. However, as these values are passed on to succeeding generations, increasing emphasis is placed on belief in and acceptance of these values, but less and less is there adherence to and expression of these values in life. Emphasis is placed on belief rather than life.

Religion becomes institutionalized when the "spirit" of religion is lost and only the form remains. Worship may be taken as an example. The true spirit of worship may be found both in a highly liturgical service of worship or in an informal service of worship. Likewise, both the liturgical or the informal service may become institutionalized; that is, the spirit may be lost and only the form remain. This principle applies also to religion in its expression in life. Expressions of religion in life, such as prayer and giving, may be outward expressions of a deep inner experience or they may be routine forms.

Religion not infrequently exhibits a tendency to become departmentalized, to move from the centre of experience to its margins. . . . Convictions become dogmas. Religious activities degenerate into meaningless and worthless forms. The institutions of religion which were the organs through which it found much of its expression and got much of its work done, become extraneous overhead organizations that lay a deadening hand upon the spirit. Finally, religion loses its moral and spiritual sensitiveness. The soul of religion is dead. In the name of God it fastens its dead weight upon progress, opposing the discovery of truth, stoning the prophets, and standing as the arch-champion of things as they are. And so it turns out that institutionalized, dogmatic, anti-social, and unethical "religion" becomes an obstacle in the way of God, crucifying His Son and defeating His purpose, so that God has had to set aside repeatedly in the course of history institutionalized forms of religion and their overzealous custodians in order to make way for the prophets of reality and the religion of the spirit.[19]

The question may be raised legitimately: If it is true that we have wandered so far from the essence of New Testament religion, why is this not apparent to more people? Indeed, why is it not apparent to all? Two answers may be given. First, this change comes about so slowly and imperceptibly one is not aware that it is happening. Evil slips in, becomes respectable, and finally is accepted as normal. The spirit and vitality which give life to religion slip away until only the external forms remain. Second, if such is the case in our day, this would not be the first time such a thing has happened in the religious life of a people and was not apparent to all—not even to the religious leaders.

In the middle of the eighth century before Christ, according to all outward appearances, religion was flourishing in Israel. It was presumed that the Israelites were pleasing to God. The people were meticulous in their observance of the sacrifices

---

[19] William Clayton Bower, *The Curriculum of Religious Education* (New York: Charles Scribner's Sons, 1925), pp. 138-139.

and other religious ceremonies. The sanctuaries throughout the land were filled with worshipers. They were living in prosperous times, a certain evidence of God's favor upon them they felt; and, in return, they were generous in their support of religion. Yet to the consternation and bewilderment of the people, the prophet Amos declared that Israel was hovering on the brink of destruction. All the outward evidences of religious success and all the outward religious displays were merely deceptive coverings for the decay that was at the heart of the nation's life. Into the midst of their smug complacency this herdsman hurled his words of doom. No wonder he aroused the hostility of the official clergy (Amos 7:10-17)! The people must have felt that here was another "fanatic" trying to disturb their situation.[20] But from the vantage point of history, we are able to understand that Amos saw what God saw, and what the religious people of that day were too blind to see; namely, that their religion was merely a beautiful shell and that the inner vitality, the inner life, was dead.

A Radical Reformation Needed

If there is any measure of accuracy in the analysis given thus far, then the situation facing modern religion is not merely serious, it is critical. "The situation, rightly seen, shakes us as a church to the very roots of our being and challenges the validity of what passes as Christianity among us."[21] There may be those who will think that this problem is only academic in nature, pursued by a seminary professor as a sort of intellectual exercise. Not so! There is no problem more serious facing religion today. It touches the very center of the life and ministry of all Christians. We seek to serve the living God, but we serve him primarily through the life and work of the church. If in any way and for any reason the church follows some other way than *the way*, then our life and ministry as Christians corre-

---

[20] James D. Smart, *The Rebirth of Ministry* (Philadelphia: The Westminster Press, 1960), p. 172.

[21] *Ibid.*, p. 162.

spondingly "misses the mark," and we are deceived at the very center of our being.

If it is true that there is a decided tendency toward institutionalism in the life of the modern church, is there any indication that the church is willing to change the pattern of its life and seek to recapture vital, experiential religion? This is not an easy question to answer. It is certainly possible for the church to do so. On the other hand, the road back to experiential religion is so difficult that the church may not be willing to pay the price. Elton Trueblood is hopeful:

> There have been different great steps at different times in Christian history, because one of the most remarkable features of the Christian faith is its ability to reform itself *from the inside*. However vigorous the outside critics of the Church may be, the inside critics, who love the movement which they criticize, are far more vigorous and searching. Reformation is not accidental or exceptional, but characteristic and intrinsic. The crust forms repeatedly, but there is always volcanic power to break through it.[22]

There is also hope in the increasing awareness and concern being evidenced by pastors and laymen alike. All the apparent success has not eliminated the disturbing fear that something is seriously wrong with the religious life of today. More and more these questions of deep concern are being raised, not by those who are hostile to the denomination or religious group, but by those who are most deeply committed to it. More and more these questions are being discussed openly in church and denominational meetings. Even now some of the churches are beginning serious and searching self-analysis. This self-appraisal will undoubtedly prove to be an agonizing experience. Where it will lead the church, no one knows.

> The whole gamut of new, stirring awareness and inner disturbance, manifested in a revival of apostolic sensitivity; of experiments in new Christian living and evangelism; of new stimulating theological thinking; . . . is the sure indication of a rising feeling that a radical Reformation of the Church is due. Probably more radical than the

---

[22] *Your Other Vocation* (New York: Harper & Bros., 1952), pp. 32-33.

Reformation of the 16th century, because the pressure both of the Spirit and of the world are upon us to rethink and reshape the response to the divine calling of the Church.[23]

If the blight of institutionalism is to be eliminated, if we are to recapture the vitality of the New Testament faith, the church must come to have a deeper and clearer understanding of herself, her life, and work. For this reason the educational program of the church, which is a primary means by which and through which the ministry of the church is realized, must rest upon a solid theological foundation. To state certain aspects of this theology, to enunciate a philosophy of education that grows out of this theology, and to suggest some practical implications of this philosophy that will serve as a guide for the life and work of the church is the purpose of this book.

This is an attempt to understand the experiential nature of New Testament Christianity and to take a serious look at ourselves in light of these findings. Certain of the proposals that will be suggested may seem to some to be drastic. Their practice did not seem so in New Testament times. They seem thus to us only because we have unconsciously wandered so far from the New Testament pattern and let ours become such a soft and easy religion. Without knowing it, we have traveled rather far down the road of institutionalism. Whether we like it or not, only drastic action will even begin to meet the seriousness of our situation. Trueblood is right in saying:

If, in this situation, one truth is more obvious than any other, it is that *we cannot win except by a radical change*. If all we have to offer is the tame routine of the conventional church, with slight improvements in technique, we might as well give up. The modern church will not make a sufficient difference by a slight improvement in the anthems or by a little better preaching or by a little better organization of the Sunday Schools. Many of these are fairly good already, but not much seems to happen, so far as the pagan order is concerned.[24]

---

[23] Kraemer, *op. cit.*, p. 99.
[24] *Op. cit.*, p. 28.

The churches today face a difficult question. Shall they continue the relatively easy type of religion which can be popular and thus appeal to the masses; or shall they submit themselves to the difficult and radical element of discipline and self-denial which was characteristic of the New Testament faith? Since the masses tend to avoid suffering, this way cannot be popular. The present generation has grown up in this popular, easy religion. Because this is all the religion they know, they tend to feel that this is what religion ought to be. But in more thoughtful moments there comes the haunting and disturbing thought that perhaps—just perhaps—the difficult way, the way of radical change, may be the only way to power, the only way to vital, experiential religion.

Thus, the church today is called upon to go through the painful process of re-evaluating herself—her essential nature, her ministry and mission in the modern world. Because of the difficulties involved these changes will come about only when, and if, the leadership of the church comes to have a deeper and clearer understanding of what the church is and what the church should be about in today's world.

The Need for Dialogue

While everyone may not agree with all the suggestions made in this book, the study can stimulate creative Christian discussion toward a more accurate understanding of God's way in the modern church. This discussion must take place in the spirit of Christ and not degenerate into unchristian controversy. Freedom to discuss and freedom to differ are fundamental aspects of vital religion. Crystallized dogmas, the denial of freedom to investigate, and the refusal to permit honest questions—all these are normative when religion has become institutionalized.

The practical proposals presented here must be viewed as working hypotheses. The writer is convinced that nothing in any denominational or organizational structure should be "torn down" until something better has first been prepared to take its place. These proposals, then, should provide the stimulation and basis for dialogue between pastors, educational workers, denominational leaders, serious laymen, college and seminary students, and others who have a genuine concern for the life and work of the churches in our time. In this dialogue there must be a persistent search for *answers*. Merely disagreeing with the proposals will make little headway in solving the problems.

The problems under study here are so serious that our analysis must be accurate and valid. It is always difficult to assess the present because it is so close to us. Because we are so personally involved in its intentions and failures, it is difficult to be objective about it. Furthermore, present experience is limited both in time and scope. For this reason, we must view the present in historical perspective. In succeeding chapters we will seek that vantage point.

Part I

The Trend Toward Institutionalism

2

How Judaism Became Institutionalized

A movement tends to go through certain rather definite stages from the time of its vigorous and dynamic inception until it becomes encrusted in a cold, lifeless formalism. Generally a movement is born in a time of great stress as a violent reaction against errors, abuses, and the injustices in the *status quo*. Its followers see it as making a positive offer to the people of a better way. It is met with open hostility, however, and often intense persecution by those who champion the *status quo*, usually the majority. With almost holy zeal those in authority seek to stamp out the movement because it is a threat to those values and to that way of life to which society has become accustomed. However, the newfound ideals, beliefs, and values are held so dear by the followers of the movement that they willingly suffer persecution rather than give them up.

If the movement is to survive this determined opposition, it must eventually organize its own institutions. This is necessary for two reasons. First, these newfound beliefs and values are so precious to followers of the movement that they have a compelling passion to share them with others. Second, some way must be found to pass on these values to succeeding generations. Otherwise, the movement would die with the passing of the first generation. Oddly enough in this early period, all is not peace and quiet even within the movement. Indeed, this period may be characterized by bitter disagreements and sharp debates concerning the beliefs and practices within the movement. Every man is free to think and to speak, for no one within the movement has the authority to compel conformity.

As the movement grows, it then becomes a hated sect, looked down upon by the society of which it is a part. This stage is characterized by zealous activity on the part of the followers of the movement, both to consolidate their present gains and to win new adherents to their point of view. The movement begins to grow rather rapidly, particularly among the down-trodden and underprivileged.

In the next stage the movement passes from rejection to toleration and finally to acceptance by society. During the passing of the years the movement influences society to some extent, and society influences the movement, so there is not now as much difference between the two as there was at the beginning. Vigorous activity in the movement leads to further growth. Then, the movement is not merely accepted, it becomes popular. The essential demands characteristic of the early movement, however, are now soft-pedaled because they are too difficult to be accepted by the masses. A taste of success convinces the leaders of the movement that the masses must be won to their "way" at almost any cost. Thus, increasingly the practice develops of teaching and explaining the demands to the adherent after he has been led to an acceptance of and commitment to this way. Also the adherents tend increasingly to develop and follow certain external forms and activities which supposedly express their loyalty to the movement. But gradually the essential spirit of the early movement is lost.

For the sake of efficiency in organization and administration, during this period of popular growth, there is a definite trend toward centralization of authority. The movement becomes so large and unwieldy, its membership so numerous and scattered, its program and activities so complex that some group will seek to unify its program and control its activities. During this period the beliefs tend to become more uniform. There is a generally accepted point of view. No centralized authority has yet de-veloped, but there is considerable group pressure that demands and leads to conformity. The nonconformist is free to go his own way if he chooses, but there are strong and subtle ways of letting it be known that he is an outsider. Thus, the pressure is quite strong upon individuals and groups to follow the accepted patterns and practices. Besides, by now the movement has a long and honorable tradition to support these practices.

How long—years, decades, or even centuries—a movement may stay in one of these stages is determined by factors both numerous and complex. These stages may not be sharply identified; at any given time in the movement there may be evidences of several different stages. All aspects of the movement do not move along uniformly. Group pressure will vie with intense efforts for freedom. Crystallized beliefs will show up along with vigorous investigation. While a majority of the followers are merely going through routine forms and keeping external observances, others will demonstrate both the zeal and the spirit of the early leaders.

Finally, we come to the last stage of the movement. Beliefs become crystallized into dogma demanding acceptance. Authority is now vested in either an individual or a group with the power to compel conformity. Heretics must be destroyed either by imprisonment or death. Since their false teachings might lead people away from the "truth," it becomes the duty of those in authority to protect the people from error. Thus acceptance of the way and conformity to its practices are expected from the people. Conformity becomes the end. The people still go through the forms, sometimes with vigor and devotion, but the spirit is lost. The movement has become encrusted with a cold, lifeless formalism—institutionalism.

Then a new movement must break through those shackles with new ideas, new beliefs, new values, and a new way. Again, those in authority will use every means of pressure and persecution to stamp out those who threaten the *status quo*. But the cycle begins anew. A new movement has started.

Learning from History

Seeking to understand, evaluate, and assess a current movement must always be done against the backdrop of history. In

one brief lifetime and in the limited observation of one person
it is impossible to get a complete picture of the whole movement. One is always too close to a current movement and too
imbued with things as they are to rely wholly upon personal experience. A movement must be viewed not only in relation to
the present but also in relation to the past. Therefore, the individual must go to the experience of the race for the amplifica-
tion of his imperfect and incomplete knowledge, for points of
view, for standards, and for techniques whereby he might
more adequately analyze and evaluate the present. Although
there are always many new elements in the race's ongoing
experience, yet a large number of the fundamental issues have
been faced by previous generations.

George Santayana, the philosopher, said, "A nation that does
not know history is fated to repeat it."[1] It is equally true that a
religious group or denomination that is not intimately ac-
quainted with Christian history and does not learn from it is
fated to repeat it; for religious movements are not exempt from
the tendency toward institutionalism. Indeed, history provides
us with alarming examples.

While the beginnings of three major religious movements
were characterized by a vital and experiential type of religion,
yet each, unaware of what was happening, went through the
usual stages into institutionalized forms. The first movement
was Judaism from Ezra and the return of the Jews from Exile
to the Pharisaism denounced during the earthly ministry of
Jesus. The second movement was Christianity from the time
of Jesus to the matured Roman Catholicism of the Middle Ages.
The third covers the period from the Reformation under Martin
Luther to the state churches in England and on the Continent.
These three movements will now be traced briefly. Within this
limited space notable exceptions to the basic pattern cannot
be included; nevertheless, that pattern does emerge in each
period. As we see how the changes took place perhaps we may

---

[1] Quoted in Edith Hamilton, "History's Great Challenge to Our Civilization,"
Reader's Digest, March, 1959, p. 160.

discover certain principles or insights that will make our analysis of the current religious situation more objective and accurate.[2]

Developing Institutions

In order to understand the Pharisaism of Jesus' day it is necessary to go back to the return of the Jews from the Exile. Here is found the beginnings of the legalistic system which determined the nature of Judaism, not only in the days of Jesus, but to the present time.[3] With the fall of Jerusalem in 586 B.C., the Jewish nation as a national power died. Religion was the only means of preserving their national distinction. Yet in the Exile many left the faith and tradition of their fathers and became absorbed in the business life of Babylon. Some saw in the sufferings and hardships of exile, however, the chastening hand of Jehovah laid upon them because of their disobedience to the law; heartily repenting, they turned with renewed devotion to the law of Moses. Concerning those in the Exile who had acknowledged their sins and had repented, Graetz says, "Those who had forsaken their evil ways in their turn converted others; former sinners showed other evil-doers the way to God. The number of the faithful, 'those who were eager for God's Word,' those 'who sought after God,' thus gradually increased." [4] A new movement was born.

Returning from the Exile, the people declared anew their devotion to the God of Abraham, Isaac, and Jacob. It was Ezra, the priest and scribe, who gave impetus and direction to this new movement. Ezra caused the observance of the law with all its feasts, fasts, sacrifices, and obligations to be supreme in the life of the people. Of course the law was not to be followed

---

[2] This is not to be understood as proposing a cyclical view of history. The biblical view of history is linear rather than cyclical. In history God is moving toward his purposes. The suggestion here is simply that religious movements in their organized expression tend to move from a period of dynamic vitality through successive stages to a period of lifeless formalism.

[3] Meyer Waxman, *A History of Jewish Literature from the Close of the Bible to Our Own Days* (New York: Bloch Publishing Co., Inc., 1930), I, 45.

[4] H. Graetz, *History of the Jews* (Philadelphia: The Jewish Publication Society of America, 1891), p. 337.

as a matter of form, but it was within the sphere of the law that the people were to find and follow the will of God. However, in this legalistic movement of Ezra the seeds are already sown for the superficial, external observance of the letter of the law that was to come into full bloom in the Pharisaism of Jesus' day. A means becomes an end.

In order for this movement, with its new found insights and deepened dedication, to be expanded among all the people and to be passed on to succeeding generations certain procedures and institutions were developed. One of the most important among these was the synagogue. Scholars are practically unanimous in agreeing that the synagogue had its origin during the Exile. It was not only a place of worship, it was also the school of the people. Its primary function was "not devotion, but religious instruction, and this for an Israelite was above all *instruction in the law.*"[5]

The rise of the order of the scribes is closely connected with the decision of the postexilic Jews to make the Torah the guide of life. It was their task to study and teach the law. Originally this was one of the functions of the priests, and many of the early scribes may have been priests. As the movement developed, however, the priests became more and more liberal in thought and practice, while the scribes became more and more zealous in their conformity to the letter of the law. Therefore, in the religious life of the people, the scribes came to wield much more influence than did the priests.

Closely associated with the scribes was the development of the oral law. The task of the scribes was stated thus in the Mishna: "Be deliberate in judgment, raise up many disciples, and make a fence around the Law."[6] But the function which increasingly dominated the work of each succeeding generation of scribes was the last: "Make a fence around the Law." To build up elaborate explanations, thorny obstructions, subtle

[5] Emil Schurer, *A History of the Jewish People in the Time of Jesus Christ* (Edinburgh: T. & T. Clark, n.d.), Div. II, II, 54.
[6] Herbert Danby (ed. and trans.) *The Mishnah.* (Fairlawn, N. J.: Oxford University Press, 1933), Aboth 1:1, p. 446.

evasions, and complex developments was the task to which the scribes gave themselves with a sense of holy dedication. By this maxim the interpreter and teacher of the law was enjoined to forbid any and all things, even though they be innocent, that touched too closely upon forbidden points in the law. This was not done with malicious intent. The scribes were just concerned that the law of God be kept in every detail. Thus these traditional interpretations in the oral law came to be more authoritative and binding than the written law itself.[7] The result was that the law of God was practically ignored in the confusion of tradition. It is no wonder that Jesus with vehemence charged: "Full well do ye reject the commandment of God, that ye may keep your tradition" (Mark 7:9, ASV).

Evidently during the three hundred years following the return of the Jews from exile the people grew lax in their devotion and obedience to the law. Institutionalism in the religious life of the people was becoming increasingly evident. Strange as it may seem, it was to stem this tide that the Pharisees came into existence. The Pharisees as a distinct party were mentioned first during the reign of John Hyrcanus. The name literally means "the separated." They became aware that the religion of the masses of people was shallow and superficial. The law of God did not hold for the masses the reverence it was due nor was it observed as it should be observed. Therefore those who became Pharisees followed the injunction, "come ye out from among them, and be ye separate." They gave themselves with deep earnestness and dedication to the strict observance of the Levitical laws. They dared to "go the second mile" in keeping the feasts, fasts, ceremonies, and sabbath observances, which to them was the law of God. Because their dedication to religion was apparent to all, their influence over the masses of the people was tremendous.

Thus, in the home, in the synagogue, in the temple, the religious nurture and development of the Jew was carried on, year after year and generation after generation. Broadly speak-

---

[7] *Ibid.*, Sanhedrin 11:3, p. 400.

ing, the Pharisees had two objectives. First, they sought to lead the people to know the law of God; second, they sought to lead the people to live by the law. It would be difficult to state two more worthy objectives. Yet, in spite of a dedicated beginning, in spite of institutions with worthy goals, in spite of well-meaning and well-intentioned efforts, their religious movement became institutionalized.

The Movement in Historical Perspective

Looking back upon their situation from the vantage point of two thousand years of subsequent history, we are able to see the true nature of their religious life with greater clarity than they were able to see it themselves. While they apparently were seeking to achieve the two objectives stated above, what was *actually* happening in their program of religious education and in their religious life?

First, they were successful in preserving Judaism as a religious system, but they lost the individual. In the beginning, Judaism was a means; for the individual to come to know God was the end. But with the passing of the years, unconsciously ends and means became switched. The individual was not the end or the object of supreme value; rather he became the means to the end. His task was to keep the feasts, fasts, and ceremonial observances which would insure the continuation of Judaism as an institution.

The clash which Jesus had with the Jewish religious leaders over sabbath observance is a clear illustration of this fact. When Jesus healed the man who was born blind (John 9:1-14) and the man by the pool of Bethesda who had an infirmity for thirty-eight years (John 5:1-9), he was severely condemned. Were there not six other days in the week when these men could have been healed? When Jesus said, "The sabbath was made for man, (Mark 2:27) and not man for the sabbath," he was seeking to help them see that their concern for their institutional sabbath observance had superseded their concern for needy individuals. Their system was preserved, but the individual was lost. There is a strong tendency for this to happen in any generation.

Second, they were successful in preserving their orthodoxy and in passing on a tradition, but they failed to appropriate to themselves a deeper understanding of God's truth. They had come to believe that their traditions, their orthodox doctrines, were all true and that they contained all the truth. Thus, the freedom to think beyond their traditions was denied. Of course they could and did have frequent differences of opinion and bitter disagreements and discussions within the tradition, but one was strictly forbidden to go outside or contrary to tradition. Those who violated or endangered it were "put out of the synagogue." By this act the individual was eternally damned and became an outcast from his family and society. His former friends and neighbors would shun him as though he had a disease. No one would hire him as a laborer, or if he had a business, no one would purchase from him. He was shorn of salvation, family, friends, and livelihood. Thus the pressure to keep within the tradition was strong.

From the perspective of the Jewish religious leaders, why should not this so-called freedom to break with tradition be denied to any man? Was it not true that within their orthodox tradition was to be found *the* way to life with God? Was it not also true that outside their tradition was condemnation and damnation? Were they not justified, then, in using every means at their disposal to keep the people within the tradition and to keep them from error that led to death? Thus, the task of religious education was to pass on this tradition, intact, from generation to generation, and to expect from every generation acceptance and obedience, for herein is life.

Then Jesus came suddenly into their midst with his revolutionary teachings. "Ye have heard that it was said by them of old time, . . . but I say unto you." Indeed, he did not teach as one of the scribes. Here was a heretic of the first order! He was threatening the very foundations upon which their traditions were built. Who did this Galilean carpenter think he was, anyway? Was not this Joseph's son? Did he think he was greater than Moses, who gave them the law? Did he think he was smarter than all the scribes who ever lived and who through the years had interpreted the meaning of the law and given them these traditions? This was presumption of the highest magnitude! This man was not only condemning himself; he was also deceiving the people and leading them to condemnation. They must save the people from this man! He must die! Was it not better that one man die than that multitudes of the people be deceived and lost?

Thus he died; and to an extent, they saved their tradition. But during the years from the time of Ezra, as the Jewish leaders passed their tradition on from generation to generation, as they preserved a purity of orthodoxy, without their being aware of it, something tragic happened. They had lost the deeper truth of God—another characteristic of institutionalized religion.

Third, they were successful in leading the people into an external conformity with the outward expressions of religion, but they failed to lead the people adequately into an inner experience with God. Religion came to be not so much a communion between God and man but a matter of keeping the feasts, the prescribed periods of prayer, the periods of fasting, and the ceremonial observances. There was little concern for the motive that might underlie these external observances.

In one of the clashes Jesus had with the Pharisees he said, "Go ye and learn what this meaneth, I desire mercy, and not sacrifice" (Matt. 9:13, ASV). Here Jesus was accusing them of ignorance of Hosea 6:6. A. T. Robertson says that the "go ye and learn" was a common formula with the rabbis, and the use of it by Jesus as a rabbi to rabbis had additional force and even some sting.[8] In effect Jesus said, "You religious leaders have studied religion and the Scriptures all your lives, but you don't know what it is all about. You have lost completely the spirit which is the essence of religion which alone gives meaning to the forms you keep."

---

[8] *The Pharisees and Jesus* (New York: Charles Scribner's Sons, 1920), p. 114.

During this period the religious life of the Jew did not proceed from an inward, spiritual motive. It was no longer the free manifestation of a deep moral concern, but a result of the external constraint of legal requirement. The only duty in religion was to fulfil to the letter the requirement of the law. All depended on the external correctness of an action. If the person was regular in his attendance at the (synagogue) services, and if he kept the religious observances, he was accepted as a religious person. The depth of his religion was measured by the number of services he attended and how carefully he kept the other religious requirements. This, to them, was what it meant to be religious.

Thus the religious life of the people among whom Jesus lived was gripped by formal and legalistic traditionalism. The letter of the Mosaic law, plus numerous traditions, had become so over-emphasized that the expression of religion was a matter of mere form. The unbearable burden of external and ceremonial observances crushed the inner dynamic and externalized the spiritual element in religion. It had become an authoritarian, legalistic system encrusted in the shell of a narrow, formal externalism.

Today we read in the Scriptures about Jesus' scathing denunciation of the scribes and Pharisees; we study in our churches evidences of how far the religion of the Jews missed the mark of the truth of God; we discuss together the shallow mockery of an external religion that followed the forms of religion but lost the spirit of it. Our condemnation of their religion is so complete that we may get the impression that it came about through the designs of scheming and malicious men. This is not true! These people had a zeal toward God. They had a passion for God. Through the years their religious leaders had interpreted for them how life ought to be lived. Their beliefs were based on the law of God. In the midst of heathenism and idolatry all about them they had held firm their faith in the one God.

Yet, after every attempt has been made to understand what

happened and how it happened; after motives have been examined and, to a large degree, exonerated; after due allowances have been made for human weaknesses and ignorance; after all explanations have ceased; the result remains the same. From the perspective of God, who sees us as we are, their religion had become institutionalized. This is one of the real dangers of institutionalism. The people involved are never really aware that it is happening to them. In fact, they are quite sure that it is not. The changes in a movement take place so gradually that they are imperceptible. Success in the institutionalized church blinds its members to its weaknesses. Because the people have never known anything else, they tend to identify religion as it is with religion as it ought to be. Religion becomes institutionalized and they know it not.

3

How Early Christianity
Became Institutionalized

Into the midst of the encrusted formalism of Judaism, Jesus came, lived, and taught. With dynamic message and creative teaching he burst through the hard crust of traditionalism that had engulfed the religion of his day and fanned the smoldering ember of dynamic, spiritual religion until it became a living fire within his followers. Ideologies as represented by the Pharisees and Jesus could not live together in the same world, for they were diametrically opposed to one another. It was not surprising, therefore, that soon after Jesus started his public ministry, the religious leaders began to seek to take his life. And well they might, for he sounded the death knell for the externalism and traditionalism in religion for which they stood.

A New Movement Is Born

Jesus held that the essence of religion was found, not in conforming to some external legal norm, but in loving God supremely and one's neighbor as one's self. But the power for living this new life was not to be found within man himself. It was necessary for man to be "born again," and Jesus said this new birth came only through faith in him. Wherever Jesus went he preached to induce people to surrender to him and his way of life—the only way to the abundant life. The reactions to Jesus and his teachings were varied. Some people loved him supremely and left all to follow him; others wondered; some doubted; still others hated him intensely.

Because of the impact of his ministry the religious leaders decided that he must die. His claims of authority and his call

for complete surrender to his way were irreconcilable with
their traditional system. One had to go. So the religious leaders
stirred up the people to clamor for Jesus' death, and between
two thieves they nailed him to a cross. They crucified the
leader; but the movement he started could not be stopped, for
it lived in the hearts and lives of men and women who were
willing to die for him.

Starting from an insignificant province and from a despised
race, proclaimed in the main by a mere handful of unlearned
men, challenging everything for which the pagan world stood,
and enduring almost unbelievable persecutions, the Christian
movement faced many obstacles. But faith in God was no
longer a matter of intellectual assent or external obedience.
Religion was now a matter of vital life experience, and neither
the might of the Roman Empire nor the wiles of Satan were
able to overcome it. Meetings and forms and ceremonies there
were, to be sure; but these were merely outward expressions
of a deep inner experience. Christianity was based upon an
experiential relationship with God in Christ.

Persecution, severe and relentless, was soon unleashed against
the followers of this Christian movement, who threatened the
religious *status quo*. In a manner incomprehensible to the religious and political leaders the early Christians met their
adversaries in a spirit of determined confidence. Theirs was the
conviction that they "must obey God rather than men" (Acts
5:29). Theirs was an inner compulsion that led them to say,
"We cannot but speak the things which we have seen and
heard" (Acts 4:20). Therefore, in the midst of persecution,
"they that were scattered abroad went every where preaching
the word" (Acts 8:4). Indeed, the blood of martyrs became the
seed of the church.

Developing Institutions

During his earthly ministry Christ founded the church as
the fellowship of the redeemed, commissioned to be instruments of God's redemptive purpose in the world. In spite of

almost intolerable opposition, the early Christian movement grew rapidly. The Spirit of Christ guided the fellowship to develop certain institutions in order to preserve and propagate the values gained in the movement. The earliest churches met in the homes of various Christians for fellowship, instruction, and simple worship. Eventually, the church services followed a more definite pattern. In the first part of the service, inquirers were allowed to attend along with the "faithful," but at a certain point in the service the inquirers were required to leave and only the "faithful" remained.

In the apostolic period, when the majority of converts were from the Jews or Jewish proselytes who were already familiar with the teachings of the Old Testament, they were received into the church by baptism after only a very brief course of instruction and upon a simple confession of faith, "Jesus Christ is Lord." However, as converts from among the heathen became more numerous during the second and third centuries, it was deemed wise, for the sake of greater unity, purity, and understanding in the church, to give candidates for baptism more extended instruction. The heathen who had just laid off his paganism for the new faith usually knew little about the background and standards of this new way of life. His background was polytheistic and immoral. He had everything to learn. The churches developed, therefore, what was known as catechumenal, or rudimentary, instruction which all Jews, heathen, and children of Christians were required to take before being received into full fellowship with the church. Through this catechumenal instruction the early church sought to insure a regenerate church membership and to insure that the principles of faith and doctrine of the Christian movement would be preserved and practiced.

This instruction did not seek mere intellectual comprehension or skilful participation in the forms and ceremonies of the church. The life lived by Christians in the church and in society showed the inquirer what was involved in becoming a Christian. In addition, this instruction helped him to understand what he was surrendering and what he was adopting in its stead. The new "way" demanded a new loyalty, changed attitudes, and a new life. This instruction was given prior to baptism. As John Fletcher Hurst points out, to help insure that the individual had learned the "lessons" in his experience and life, there was a period of probation lasting up to three years before he was received into full communion with the church.[1] It was not their knowledge that was tested; it was their life that was observed.

Toward Institutionalism

In the midst of rising heresies it became quite important that the faith be preserved in purity. But how was this to be done? Who would be best qualified to discern between truth and error? Who, indeed, but one of the bishops of the church in the large city, which served as the base for evangelizing the surrounding territory? But which bishop? In the early churches there was a plurality of bishops. Among these bishops, one tended to rise to the top by virtue of dedication, native ability, and qualities of leadership. By the second century, this one came to be known as the monarchical bishop. What choice could be more logical or natural than for the monarchical bishop to be the one to discern between orthodoxy and heresy? Did he not know the faith better than anyone else? Thus, the responsibility for confirmation came to be placed in the hands of the monarchical bishop. No one could become a member of the congregation without his approval.[2]

If it was important that the membership preserve the purity of faith, it was even more important that the church ordain as preachers and teachers only those who were pure in the faith. Who was better qualified for this important responsibility than the monarchical bishop? Therefore, in time, the right of

---

[1] *History of the Christian Church* (New York: Eaton and Mains, 1897), I, 342-344.

[2] Ignatius, Epistle to the Smyrnaeans. Quoted in Henry Bettenson (ed.), *Documents of the Christian Church* (New York: Oxford University Press, 1947), pp. 89-90.

ordination was also reserved to this bishop. If a person wanted to become a member of the church, or if a young man wanted to be ordained to the ministry, he must make sure that his doctrines did not incur the displeasure or condemnation of the monarchical bishop. That the purity of the faith had to be preserved and that those bishops were probably best qualified to do it cannot be denied. Nevertheless, we have here the first steps toward centralized authority.

Often when a person became a Christian, all orthodox Jews would boycott his business, or if he were a laboring man, he could find no one who would give him a job. Thus, in the early church many members faced serious financial need. In addition, traveling evangelists often needed financial assistance. To meet these and similar needs, the churches shared with those in need. Special collections were taken. Soon funds were built up for these emergencies.

Who would be the person best qualified to keep this fund and dispense it wisely? Who would be most trusted in the community? Who, indeed, but the monarchical bishop? Thus, if a family needed financial help, they must make sure that in no way, either doctrinally or otherwise, had they offended the bishop. The traveling evangelist who expected financial help from a church must make sure that he was on the good side of this bishop. The individual or the group who controls the dispensing of financial assistance has one of the most powerful of all weapons to control both people and program. Thus, the trend toward centralized authority continued.[3]

Among the monarchical bishops, it was only natural that those in the large centers and those most capable should come

---

[3] There were efforts at reform even within the early church. Marcion is sometimes referred to as the first church reformer. The Marcionites, ca. 135, though they had some Gnostic tendencies, were primarily a group who reacted against the growing institutionalism in the church. The Montanists, ca. 150, sought to give renewed emphasis to the charismatic element in the life of the church and in this connection sought to magnify the work of the Holy Spirit. The Novatians, ca. 250, and the Donatists, ca. 315, rebelled against the growing laxity and immorality in the church. They emphasized a form of puritanism in daily life.

to have a place of influence over the others. By the third century there had developed the diocesan bishop, and by the fourth century there were the metropolitan bishops. Among these metropolitan bishops, five, known as the patriarchs, came to be dominant: the bishops at Jerusalem, Antioch, Alexandria, Constantinople, and Rome. Finally, by the fifth century the bishop of Rome had gained a clear supremacy over the others, and non-Catholic historians generally date the beginning of the Roman Catholic Church from this period.[4]

Many and great pressures worked from within and without to contribute to this growing tendency toward hierarchy and toward a changed conception of the church and its function. Changes also took place in education. In A.D. 529 the Emperor Justinian ordered the closing of all pagan schools, including the universities, and the Roman Catholic Church became the sole agent of education. This fact lies at the very heart of any understanding of the Middle Ages. It explains why the Roman Catholic Church had such a tremendous hold over the life of the people. The agent of education—who determines what shall be taught and how it shall be taught—largely determines thereby what kind of person the individual shall become.

Education became more and more authoritarian. As early as A.D. 325, at the Council of Nicaea, there was drawn up a test for teachers to which the bishops, who were the official teachers, had to subscribe. "Its purpose was thus to distinguish between teachers, and to sever orthodox from erroneous and Catholic from heretic." [5] Naturally, with the rise of this authoritarian education, the spirit of free inquiry and creative investigation began to decline. Kurtz says that the middle of the fifth century, and particularly the Council of Chalcedon, may be regarded as the turning point. After this the spirit of independent research gradually disappeared.

---

[4] Some scholars give a later date. Cf. Penrose St. Amant, "Roman Catholic Church," *Encyclopedia of Southern Baptists* (Nashville: Broadman Press, 1958), II, 1170-1172.

[5] B. J. Kidd, *A History of the Church to A.D. 461* (Fair Lawn, N. J.: Oxford University Press 1922), I, 259).

Political oppression, hierarchical exclusiveness, narrowing monasticism, and encroaching barbarism choked all free scientific effort, and the industry of compilers took the place of fresh youthful intellectual production. The authority of the older church teachers stood so high and was regarded as binding in so eminent a degree that the Council's argument was carried on almost solely by means of quotations from the writings of those fathers who had been recognized as orthodox.[6]

One cannot help but be reminded of the Pharisees in the time of Jesus who found their authority in appealing to the orthodox rabbis of the past.

The church survived the period of intense persecution. It grew rapidly in spite of the rigid requirements demanded of its adherents and in spite of being a despised sect. In A.D. 313 the Edict of Milan gave legal status to Christianity for the first time. In 323 Constantine, who had become a nominal Christian, became sole emperor, and suddenly Christianity achieved a status it had never known before. Masses of people became Christian because it was the popular thing to do. Under Theodosius, Christianity became the state religion of the Roman Empire in A.D. 380.

Since Christianity had become so popular, and since so many new members were being brought into the church, it was impossible to give the catechumenal instruction to all who had been "converted." Therefore, this preliminary instruction was gradually dropped, and the training which had preceded baptism was now placed *after* the rite. It is quite possible that this practice, with all that is implicit in it, was one powerful factor that led away from the idea of a regenerate church membership and led eventually toward institutionalism in religion.

The church seemed to make little effort to touch the experience of the individual and change his character. The test of a good church member was his assent to a body of doctrine. His orthodoxy rather than his conduct was central. The experiential,

---

[6] Johann Heinrich Kurtz, *Church History* (New York: Funk & Wagnalls Co., 1888), I, 276-277.

creative faith of the early church degenerated into an intellectual acceptance of dogma among the intelligent, and credulity and superstition among the masses.

No one person or group with malicious intent brought about this changed view of the church. It came about gradually in the attempt of the church to adjust herself to and overcome the tremendous pressures that were exerted upon her from without and within. Neither did any one person or group with malice aforethought bring about this changed concept of education. It was the natural outgrowth of the changes that had taken place within the church. Be that as it may, these changes opened the door for many of the evils that were to come in and plague the church during the latter half of the Middle Ages.

The Movement in Historical Perspective

As we are now able to look back upon this situation from the vantage point provided by history, what were some of the results of these changes in the church and in education that had come about so gradually over the centuries? In the first place, religion for the individual was no longer a matter of life and experience but a matter of form and ceremony. Salvation was no longer a matter of relationship with Christ in which the individual was transformed into a new creature. Now the individual was born into the Roman Church. He was saved and sustained in his Christian life by the sacraments of the Church. Many of the clergy accentuated this externalism in religion by encouraging the people to rely on absolution and indulgences rather than impressing upon them the necessity of true repentance of the heart.

Worship, which is the intimate communion of man with his God, became increasingly ritualistic and formal. The worship service itself was conducted in a language the people did not understand, and often the priest did not know the meaning of the words he recited. But this was of no consequence, since the blessing and virtue came through the act of receiving communion regardless of the understanding and the heart attitude of the individual involved. Prayer, which to the early Christians was a rich personal experience of fellowship with God, came to be a repetition of a prayer form. And the blessing was expected, not through the communion of the spirit of the individual with the divine Spirit, but through the mere repetition of the prayer.

In the second place, the type of authoritarian, transmissive education which was practiced preserved orthodoxy at the expense of creativity. To preserve traditional dogma was more important than to find truth, and often the zeal of the church hindered truth because it did not coincide with tradition. The church gave the authoritarian interpretation of the Bible, and no other interpretation was tolerated. Of course, it was with benevolent intent that the Roman Church bound the people by this kind of education. The church assumed that it had final truth. Therefore, it must govern what the people learned, for to learn anything contrary was to learn something false and could lead only to eternal damnation. Error had no right to exist. Since the church already had the truth, final and complete, stifling creative inquiry was a small price to pay to insure that error would not threaten the life of the people. Thus, by authoritarian education and by the powerful weapon of excommunication, the church preserved its orthodoxy. Creativity and freedom were lost, and faith degenerated into a mere intellectual acceptance of the traditional dogmas.

The third primary result of the education of this period was the preservation of the institution of the Roman Catholic Church. When all else was crumbling, authoritarian education preserved the church. But it preserved the institution at the expense of the individual. The education that was given in the schools was "intended to meet the needs of an institution rather than of a people, and to prepare those who studied in them for service to that institution." [7] Education was of the church, by the church, and for the church. The common people lived in

---

[7] Ellwood P. Cubberley, *The History of Education* (New York: Houghton Mifflin Co., 1920), p. 172.

ignorance. Training was given only for the clergy. These were taught to read that they might study the Bible; to write that they might make copies of the sacred books and of the psalter; to sing that they might take part in the chants at the religious services; to learn arithmetic that they might calculate the return of Easter and other church festivals.[8]

There is certainly nothing innately wrong in preserving an institution. Institutions are necessary to the life of any movement. The tragedy comes when the institution becomes the end in itself rather than the means to an end. That is exactly what happened in this period. The Roman Catholic Church became the all-absorbing end, and the individual was forgotten. The church no longer existed for the people; the people existed for the church.

Once again the cycle toward institutionalism had run its course. Religion had become primarily external and ceremonial in nature. The individual was held in the strong, cold hand of an authoritative ecclesiasticism. Forms stiffened into fetters; the shell was mistaken for the kernel; the means became ends in themselves. Already one might hear the rumblings of the movement that soon was to break through this encrustation; a movement that emphasized individual freedom and true faith as commitment.

---

[8] Elmer Harrison Wilds, *The Foundations of Modern Education* (New York: Farrar & Rinehart, Inc., 1936), p. 178.

4

From the Reformation
to the Present

Only a revolution could break through the hard shell of the authoritarian Roman Catholic system. Among others, the Waldenses, Wycliffe, and Huss attempted to break out of this encrustation, but they were ruthlessly suppressed. The Roman Church, however, could not completely destroy the growing spirit of freedom. Within its imposing ecclesiastical system there was a force—a struggling for freedom, and its force gradually acquired sufficient strength to break through the walls that confined it. Fundamentally, the clash was between the forces representing the authority of the church as opposed to the authority of the Bible, and salvation through the church as opposed to salvation through personal faith. The Reformation was a movement to recapture the inner spirit of religion so that religion might be vital, personal, and experiential, rather than a matter of conformity to external forms of religion.

A New Movement Is Born

The fundamental principles of the Reformation were: (1) justification by faith, (2) the Scriptures as the only rule of faith and practice, (3) the priesthood of all believers. These principles evidence the rediscovery of the individual; they stress both the competency and the freedom of the individual. In the beginning of this movement, religion and education once again put the individual in his rightful place as the end of all endeavor, the unit of supreme worth.

The theological principle that salvation is by personal faith carried with it a significant implication for the educational task of the church. If salvation comes only through the exercise of an intelligent, personal faith, then it is highly important that all be taught to read so that they are able to read the Bible for themselves and to understand its meaning for their own lives. Thus, in making each individual responsible for his own salvation, the Reformation contracted the serious responsibility of placing each individual in the condition whereby he might work out his own salvation through a study of the Bible. Education in the Roman Church had been intended only for the clergy, while the great mass of people were left in ignorance. Now this new principle of salvation by faith meant that education had to be given to all the people and that the Bible had to be translated so that the people might be able to read it.

Also, a new concept of the nature of revealed truth brought a changed view of individual freedom. The Roman Church looked upon religion as "a completed truth, revealed in its entirety by divine providence and given into the hands of an institution, whose origin, constitution, and authority are divine in the same sense and for the same reason that obtain in the case of the original revelation." [1] The Reformation held that the revelation in Christ was a perfect and complete revelation of truth, but the particular meaning of the principles of this truth, in time and place, is given by the application of each man's reason to the original revelation under the leadership of the Holy Spirit. If the first view is accepted, then only a select few need to receive education for these principles and interpretations of truth are final, complete, and unchanging for all time, and they need only to be handed down in "package form" to each succeeding generation. They do not need to be studied and understood; they need only to be accepted. But if the second view is accepted, if each individual is to know what this truth means for him in his own life and experience, then individual freedom without external coercion or pressure is an absolute necessity.

---

[1] Paul Monroe, A *Text-Book in the History of Education* (New York: The Macmillan Co., 1905), p. 402.

Thus the reformers claimed for themselves both the freedom to go back to the original sources for authority and the freedom of each individual to interpret these sources. It was not only the right, but the responsibility of every individual to interpret the Scriptures according to his own reason under the leadership of the Spirit of God. On both these principles Luther based his case before the Diet at Worms in 1521. Asked whether he would recant part of the things he had published in his books he replied,

Unless I am convicted by Scripture or by right reason (for I trust neither in Popes nor in Councils, since they have often erred and contradicted themselves)—unless I am thus convinced, I am bound by the texts of the Bible, my conscience is captive to the Word of God, I neither can nor will recant anything, since it is neither right nor safe to act against conscience. God help me. Amen.[2]

Again, he had some strong words concerning the freedom of interpretation: "It belongs to each and every Christian to know and to judge of doctrine, and belongs in such wise that he is *anathema* who shall have diminished this right by a single hair." [3] Thus, theoretically at least, "the Scriptures were no longer a closed treasury of truth and grace of which ortho-dox learning alone held the key, but an open garden, in which any devout soul might wander, plucking flowers and fruit." [4]

The logical outcome of the Reformation principles as stated by Luther and others would have provided a movement that was capable of continuous progress, expansion, and change. Granting individual freedom, these principles left room for differences of opinion and for change; each individual was to interpret revealed truth for himself in the light of changed and changing conditions. They made it possible for religion to re-

---

[2] Ernest Carroll Moore, *The Story of Instruction: the Church, the Renais-sances, and the Reformations* (New York: The Macmillan Co., 1938), II, 493-494.

[3] Charles Beard, *The Reformation of the Sixteenth Century in Its Relation to Modern Thought and Knowledge* (London: Williams and Northgate, 1897), p. 124.

[4] *Ibid.*, p. 120.

main vital and experiential, for they gave to every man the privilege and freedom to investigate and experience religion for himself and to live it according to his own convictions under the Spirit. But, unfortunately, it is one thing to lay down general principles; it is another to follow them faithfully in all their practical applications. It is one thing to claim freedom for one's self, another to accord that same freedom to others.

Toward Institutionalism

The principle that each individual was to have the freedom to interpret the Scriptures according to his own reason did not work out in actual practice. In fact, it was completely reversed before the end of a single generation. While making his fight against the Pope, Luther declared, "It is admitted that reason is the chief of all things, and among all that belongs to this life, the best, yea, a something divine." [5] That was when Luther himself was doing the reasoning. Later, when his own position was threatened, he swung to the opposite extreme and wrote, "The more subtle and acute reason is, the more poisonous a beast it is, with many dragons' heads; it is against God and all His works." [6] Thus, he committed the grave error of refusing to others the same liberty and freedom he demanded for himself.

Is this error inescapable for frail human nature? Is it possible for a religious group to believe sincerely that it has the truth which leads to life and still grant to every group member the freedom of investigation that entails the possibility the individual may come to conclusions which differ from those held by the group? The answer of history is no. But history also says that such an attitude is an absolute essential for experiential religion.

The freedom which the Reformation had promised to the individual was realized neither in religion nor in education. In-

---

[5] Monroe, *op. cit.*, pp. 403-404.

[6] Frank Pierrepont Graves, *A History of Education During the Middle Ages and the Transition to Modern Times* (New York: The Macmillan Co., 1910), II, 204.

stead, an authoritarian education almost as stereotyped and formal as any that existed in the Middle Ages came into being. Traditional transmissive education continued. Nominally, the state became the agent in education, but actually the Protestant state churches controlled and directed education. The agency in education was simply transferred from the Roman Church to Protestant leadership, and the Protestant control was as domineering and authoritarian as the Catholic had ever been. The teachers were chosen according to their orthodoxy and their conformity to the accepted religious practices.

The church was supposed to be the means by which the individual was to find God in his own experience, according to his own reason and the dictates of his heart. It soon became evident, however, that the people existed for the churches and not the churches for the people. The principle that "religion goes with the land" was dominant, especially in Germany. The celebrated Peace of Augsburg granted religious freedom only to the rulers, and they were given only one alternative. The people had to practice and support the religion of the ruler regardless of their personal feelings or beliefs. Likewise, in England the people did not choose the church; they were born into it.

Education had two main aims—orthodoxy in belief and conformity in practice. Seeking to maintain a *status quo* and their own theological distinctiveness, the churches aimed more at conformity on the part of the people rather than at experiential religion. Although Luther never identified saving faith with orthodox belief, his followers were not so careful. Melanchthon held that the church was composed "of those who hold pure doctrine and agree in it." [7] The Lutheran theologians came to hold that the acceptance of the Formula of Concord was necessary to salvation, "because it set forth the true interpretation of the Bible." [8]

---

[7] Arthur Cushman McGiffert, *Protestant Thought Before Kant* (New York: Charles Scribner's Sons, 1911), p. 77.
[8] *Ibid.*, pp. 144-145.

By their highhanded methods and authoritarian education the churches on the Continent and in England achieved to some extent their aims. But in choosing a transmissive education for handing on to succeeding generations the benefits of the Reformation, the leaders were actually sounding the death knell of the movement. It was meant to bring virility and life; instead it brought stagnation and death. The Reformation had largely abandoned its mission, it had lost its distinctive principle. Education once again became stereotyped, traditional, and authoritarian. Religion once more became bound in the hard shell of institutionalism.

The Baptist Movement

Underneath the shell of authoritarian religion as represented by the state churches which sought external conformity by the use of force if necessary, there were still a few brave spirits who dared to worship God according to the dictates of their own conscience and who dreamed of the time when all men would be granted this privilege. Out of this situation the free church movement was born.

Baptists, as a self-conscious denomination, had their beginnings in the early part of the seventeenth century, and since 1641 Baptist doctrine and practice have been the same in essential features as they are today.[*] At least two distinctive principles marked the Baptist movement from its beginning. First, Baptists vigorously opposed infant baptism and insisted upon believer's baptism only and a regenerate church membership. Second, they advocated religious freedom—the right of every man to worship God as he saw fit. In justification of their position Baptists appealed to the authority of the Bible as opposed to the tradition of the church.

In England people who held these Baptist views faced dire difficulties because of the Established Church and its traditional social prestige and power and its sacramental and sacer-

---

[*] It is not my intent here to raise the question of when Baptists originated. For this reason I use the phrase, "as a self-conscious denomination."

dotal conceptions of Christianity. Thus, as is the case at the beginnings of all movements, Baptists met with rank intolerance and severe persecution. However, religion for these people was a vital, dynamic experience and would not and could not be bound by the traditional forms of the Established Church.

The Baptist movement spread to America when, in order to escape this intense persecution, many who had separated from the Established Church migrated to the New World in search of religious toleration and freedom. But they were doomed to disappointment, for several established churches already dominated the colonies; many religious groups who demanded religious freedom for themselves refused to grant that same right to others. The resulting severe persecution cast a dark shadow across the pages of colonial religious history. Baptists and others of similar conviction led the fight to secure freedom of worship not only for themselves but for all people. Rhode Island, under the leadership of Roger Williams, a Baptist, was the first colony whose charter guaranteed absolute religious freedom so long as its exercise did not disturb public order.

Baptists now seem to have gone through the following stages: (1) Out of the formal religion as represented by the state churches a vital movement burst forth. Met by severe and persistent persecution, the movement had sufficient vitality and strength not only to survive but also to grow. (2) While developing its institutions, the movement consolidated its gains and propagated its distinctive values. (3) Eventually, it became a significant sect although misunderstood and rejected by society. In spite of this, its adherents were so zealous that this period was characterized by rather rapid growth, particularly among the poor and underprivileged. (4) Baptists gradually came to be accepted by society while the movement was still characterized by a vigorous vitality. Growth during this period was primarily among the middle class and the working man. (5) Focusing our attention now on Southern Baptists, the denomination is not only accepted, it is popular.

Its growth has been rapid and remarkable.[10] Membership in the churches and in all the organizations of the churches is increasing. New churches are being built in ever increasing numbers. Church budgets are at an all-time high.

If the three great religious movements we have considered can serve as any criteria, it would seem that Southern Baptists have gone approximately halfway through the cycle. As a denomination they stand at the crossroads. For this reason it is tremendously important for them to take a frank and serious look at themselves to analyze and evaluate the present, that they might more adequately and more intelligently chart the future.

Self-analysis and Self-evaluation

From its inception the Baptist movement was characterized by a promising vitality—a movement of the people, by the people, and for the people. It granted freedom to the individual. It was nonecclesiastical. It insisted upon the separation of church and state. It was nonauthoritarian, democratic, biblical, and experiential. Thus, Baptists seem to have all the basic qualities to encourage a growing, expanding, dynamic movement.

As we contemplate the immediate future, the problem is this: Will the Baptist movement go on and complete the cycle of encrustation so that new life will have to break out and form a new evangelical movement, or is it possible for it to exercise intelligent, purposive control to continue to be a growing, ex-

---

[10] In this analytical evaluation I turn my attention to my own religious group, Southern Baptists, because it is the group with which I am most familiar. An analysis of this type, which at points may seem to be somewhat critical in nature, should be made by one who is within the group, who identifies himself with the group and accepts his share of responsibility for whatever weakness there may be in the group. Further, the time has come when we need to be much more specific in our thinking and in our analysis. The cause of Christianity in the United States will be better served if those in the various religious groups would become more specifically concerned about the quality and expression of the religious life of the group with which they are immediately identified. For this reason I do not attempt to relate what is said here to any other religious group.

panding movement, using institutions without becoming institutionalized?

We are living in a crisis period. Whether we will be able to give an adequate witness in our generation is open to real question. For this reason the time has come for a careful and penetrating analysis. There are tendencies and practices in the life of our denomination where red flags of warning need to be raised. Some aspects of our program need to be examined carefully with spiritual concern *now* before they become crystallized; for once they have become crystallized, change will be exceedingly difficult, if not impossible.

Success is the basic characteristic of the stage of the cycle in which we find ourselves, and success can be one of the most serious of all threats to experiential religion. Numerical growth is not always the result of, or even an evidence of, experiential religion. Our program of religious education is highly successful, but is it making religion vital and experiential in the lives of people, or is religion tending more and more to become merely adherence to a creed and conformity to external forms? Is this program leading people to believe that attending church meetings and tithing constitute the core of Christianity? It will not do to answer the challenge of these questions by condemning one who dares to raise such questions. Nor can we answer them in terms of past achievement or appeal to loyalty founded on sentiment. These are questions far too important to be scoffed at or merely brushed aside.

Our denomination has genuine vitality and it must not be lost. It is a crucial quality of a dynamic movement. But vitality must be given both direction and structure for effective implementation. At this point a danger arises. Professor James E. Tull discusses this problem in an article entitled, "Responsible Denominationalism." By responsible denominationalism he means "the dedicated, mature, and intelligent attention which a denomination should give to its own stewardship of the gospel." Because of the incisive nature of his analysis a somewhat extended passage is given:

We should seek a more adequate understanding of the relationship between the vital and the structural elements of our denominational life. . . .

The function of the formal, the institutional, the structural is to furnish a channel for the communication of the Spirit. Structural and institutional forms are therefore never ultimate in themselves. They are under the judgment of the Spirit. Always the test of structure is whether it furnishes a proper home for the Spirit, whether it remains pliant to the will of the Spirit, whether it is kept transparent, so that the Spirit shines through.

A prime danger of structural form is that it sometimes assumes the place of spiritual content. When this happens, a debasement of meaning occurs. Legitimate form becomes formalism; promotion becomes promotionalism; the institutional gives place to institutionalism. Then the grindings of the structural machinery are misconceived to be the movings of the Spirit. The synchronized turnings of denominational engines are thought to be the mighty stirrings of the Spirit of God. . . .

A maturely responsible denominationalism requires us to remember that we have a confessing faith, not a possessing faith. We do not possess God; we confess him. We do not possess the great verities of our faith; we confess them. Repeatedly, the structural form has been used as a device for capturing the Spirit, and for holding it as a possession. Disaster results, for it is a common lesson of history that the gospel is often lost specifically among those who are its most striking advocates. And God's Spirit, leaving the smoothly working forms which have been prepared for him, seeks out other structures which are more responsive to his will. Unfortunately, no outward sign betrays his departure, for the structural wheels roll as efficiently under the driving of an alien spirit as they do under the jurisdiction of God's Spirit.

A prayerful and searching examination of the institutional structures of our denominational life, to see whether they are open to the Spirit, is our paramount and perennial task.[11]

In a manner that is quite remarkable, the program of religious education as devised and practiced by Southern Baptists *works*. It is eminently successful. It has passed the pragmatic test. Let there be no misunderstanding at this point. *Methods are not to be condemned because they are successful*. Success-

---

[11] *The Baptist Program*, May, 1959, pp. 3-4.

ful methods may be instruments of the Spirit of God. For these we are indeed grateful. The pragmatic test, however, cannot be the only consideration in determining what methods or program should be used in our organizations. It is just at this point that some questions need to be raised and some serious thinking needs to be done. One who is sensitive to this problem comments,

Southern Baptists, of course, have never subscribed to a philosophical pragmatism, such as that of Dewey. Undoubtedly, however, we often have proceeded on basically pragmatic assumptions. We have developed methods in church and denominational work from experience. Our standard for employing and recommending these methods very often has not been any real consideration of their relationship to some system of ideal values, Christian or otherwise, but the simple fact that the methods have been found to work. There seems little reason to doubt that many Southern Baptist methods work so well because workability was the major reason for selecting them.[12]

The emphasis being made here is simply this: Methods, procedures, and programs may be successful but at the same time may *not* be instruments of the Spirit of God. If and when this is true in the life and work of any religious group, it needs to be faced frankly and changes made accordingly. Pragmatism does not have its roots in biblical revelation; "by their fruits ye shall know them" and "does it work" are not the same thing. Pragmatism asks only, "does it work?" For example certain techniques may work well in business, but the Spirit of God may not be able to work through these methods to accomplish the spiritual purposes of God. Business simply asks, "How can we sell more tubes of toothpaste, more boxes of soap?" But the church has more fundamental questions to ask.

After the church program has been "sold," after the people have come to the meeting, and after the awards have been earned; have the people come to a deeper understanding of the

[12] Joseph F. Green, Jr., "Theory or Practice," *The Baptist Program*, September, 1959, p. 3.

purpose for which they were called as Christians? Have they increasingly yielded themselves to be instruments of God to be used by him in his redemptive purpose? Has the church become more truly the church? This is the test the church must use in evaluating the effectiveness of its activities and program. The pragmatic test, which is founded on a humanistic world view, is not an adequate test for the Christian church. Business is concerned only with results. The church must also be concerned with motive and inner spirit. Business is concerned with profits, the church with persons.

On the other hand, just because certain methods are successful does not at all mean that they are thereby evil or unchristian. The fundamental test of any method or program for churches is not whether it is successful, but whether in fact and in reality it is accomplishing the spiritual purpose for which it was intended. Otherwise, a program that is successful without accomplishing the true spiritual purposes for which it was designed is simply filling churches with twentieth century Pharisees, and both individuals and churches deceive themselves into thinking they are something they are not.

The three religious movements studied earlier indicate clearly that one evidence of creeping institutionalism in any religious group is the tendency for individuals, churches, and denominations to become increasingly content with external evidences of success and to become increasingly less insistent on an evidence of an inner spiritual transformation and experience. The latter is more difficult to evaluate. It is certainly more difficult to achieve in the life and work of churches. Thus the temptation is almost overwhelming upon pastors and church workers to become satisfied with external evidences of success and simply to hope that the spiritual transformation has, or will, come. History teaches that when the church is most successful, it is tempted to "let down the bars" so that it may reach even more people and, in the process, become satisfied with something that is other than or less than Christian. External success may hide inner weakness.

Religious Education in a Theological Orientation

For this reason the church must always make sure that it sees and understands clearly its task in light of the spiritual purposes of God. Therefore, theology, philosophy of education, and the educational program of a church must be intimately related. The function of theology is to interpret the gospel and thus to identify the task which the church should be about. A philosophy of religious education must rest upon theology for a statement of objectives and seek to enunciate basic principles designed to achieve these objectives, consistent with the theology. The educational program of the church is the practical implementation of the educational philosophy. "To be a theologian in education is therefore to ask whether what we are doing educationally is in its central features and in all its details what we are compelled to do in faithfulness to the gospel of Jesus Christ." [13]

Religious education, by its very nature, is primarily concerned with the forms, the structure, the means, and the techniques of communicating the biblical revelation, but these are meaningless without a clear and deep awareness of that revelation. Religious education is always a means and not an end. It is the Christian faith that is shared and it is this faith that must be kept at the center. Thus, the norm is the revelation, and this norm must control the "program" which implements it. Neither a philosophy of religious education nor the educational program of the church has a firm foundation upon which to stand unless it is constructed within a theological orientation.

Theology has at least a twofold responsibility in the life and work of the church and, thus, a twofold relationship to religious education. The first responsibility is interpretation. It is the task of theology to interpret the essential nature, meaning, and purpose of the gospel for the life of the church. In this interpretative task theology must influence the educational program of the church in at least two major areas.

---

[13] Smart, *op. cit.*, pp. 108-109.

First, theology must give direction to religious education in the area of objectives. Those who lead in the educational work of the church must understand clearly the essential nature of the Christian enterprise. God has acted in human history. He has gathered and is gathering unto himself a redeemed people. He has charged his church to be the instrument of his redemptive purpose. Those who serve his church must see clearly what their spiritual objectives are in light of what God has done and is doing. Where there is confusion as to objectives or where objectives are something less than Christian, activity, however vigorous it may be, will lead only to further confusion and perhaps to tragic consequences.

Also the methods of religious education must be in harmony with the Christian gospel. Because we are seeking a spiritual end does not mean that we are free to use any legitimate means. This is to say, we do not reject means only when they are evil. Sometimes we reject means, even when they are good and legitimate, simply because they do not give us the *spiritual* end the church is seeking. Certain techniques may get church members to follow the "forms" of being Christian, but this is not the essential purpose of the Christian enterprise. Thus, the methods of religious education must always be evaluated in terms of the spiritual purposes they are designed to achieve. Regardless of the seeming external achievements of the church, if the motives of men be not Christian the church is traveling the sure road toward institutionalism and decay.

The second responsibility of theology in the life of the church is judgment. Theology exercises the function of criticism in the highest meaning of that term. Since it is the discipline that seeks to understand the Christian gospel in the depth and fulness of its meaning, it has the responsibility of constantly evaluating what the church is doing to make sure that it is being true to the gospel. Or, as Karl Barth puts it, the responsibility of dogmatics is to hear and proclaim the Word of God, and only that church can proclaim the Word which has taken the pains to hear it. Thus, theology must call attention to blind spots, omissions, failures, and errors in the life and work of the church. Religious leaders need to make certain that the gospel they teach and "promote" is not something less than the full, complete, and comprehensive gospel. They need periodically to re-examine the gospel to make sure that their understanding and interpretation of it and the response of people to it are in harmony with the revelation of God in Jesus Christ.

Fortunately, there is some evidence of a growing recognition among us that the educational work of the church must be thoroughly grounded in this theological orientation. For instance, in *The Curriculum Guide* the objectives of the church's educational program were formulated from a theological perspective.[14] Of course other steps must be taken in this direction, but this one is highly significant in that it indicates even clearer recognition that religious education and theology must be wedded.

An Experiential Philosophy of Religious Education

Baptists claim to hold certain principles which are distinctive; yet they have not formulated and enunciated a distinctive educational philosophy in harmony with these distinctive beliefs and designed to insure achievement of our spiritual purpose.

With the rise of the Sunday school movement at the close of the eighteenth century, Baptists and other religious groups followed a transmissive philosophy of education in teaching religion. This was continued until the beginning of the twentieth century when a new "creative" educational philosophy evolved. Because this creative education was usually identified in religious circles with a liberal theology, Southern Baptists in general condemned both the theology and the educational philosophy.

Some who were responsible for religious education in the denomination, however, began to feel that the traditional,

---

[14] Clifton J. Allen and W. L. Howse (eds.) *The Curriculum Guide* (Nashville: Convention Press, issued annually).

transmissive education was not achieving desired results. They recognized that there were some real values in the "creative" approach to education. They also felt that they could utilize some of the creative principles and methods without following the liberal theology. Slowly and hesitatingly they began to borrow from this newer philosophy of education. One writer, though speaking to Protestants in general, points up the problem Southern Baptists share with other religious groups.

The weakness of Christian education in recent years has been just this—that in going to secular education and other foundation disciplines like psychology and sociology for assistance, the church has allowed itself to be tragically influenced, even invaded, by their secular philosophies. So subtle has been this invasion, indeed, that the church has in recent years moved back and forth between Christian faith and pragmatism or humanism without actually being aware of its inconsistency.[15]

The result is confusion, and the work of religious education in our churches moves haltingly and does not achieve the desired spiritual results.

Without question there are definite values to be found in both the creative and transmissive approaches to religious education. However, this book proposes an educational philosophy in harmony with and, indeed, growing out of the distinctive beliefs and principles of Baptists. No claim is made concerning its originality because I am debtor to many from the past and present. Nor is any claim made that this is a completely new point of view peculiar only to Baptists; for many in other groups are in agreement with many of the positions stated herein.

"Transmissive philosophy" indicates a content-centered approach. "Creative philosophy" suggests progressive, pupil-centered education. This book offers an "experiential philosophy" of religious education. The reason for the name is quite simple. It is a philosophy of education that recognizes the place

---

[15] Rachel Henderlite, *Forgiveness and Hope* (Richmond: John Knox Press, 1961), p. 19.

and importance of personal experience both in theology and in education.

First, it places primary emphasis on the conversion experience. The experiential philosophy holds that salvation and entrance into the kingdom of God are possible only through a free, conscious, voluntary experience of an individual with Christ and a response to his demands. No program of training, regardless of how religious it may be, and no program of education, regardless of how moral it may be, can "create" a Christian. Thus creative education at its very center is a misnomer because it makes a claim it cannot fulfil. One becomes a Christian only as he comes into a living relationship with God on the basis of personal encounter with Jesus Christ.

Second, it holds to the principle of a regenerate church membership. The position here is that a true experiential type of religion can be achieved and maintained only within the framework of a regenerate church membership.

Third, it seeks to give adequate consideration to the present, on-going experience of individuals, while at the same time recognizing that individual experience can be adequately analyzed and evaluated only in terms of the incarnation—the revelation of God in Christ—and the Bible.

Fourth, it seeks to utilize the test indicated by Jesus, "By their fruits ye shall know them" (Matt. 7:20). That is, the results of religious education must be demonstrated in experience. Here the primary purpose is not to create a social ethic or a certain type of society. It is simply that a personal experience (encounter) with God *makes* a person live a certain way in society. The Christian changes society because he is changed. As a Christian his primary purpose is to do the will of God, and in so doing both he and society are changed.

Fifth, the experiential philosophy of religious education is based upon the concept of individual responsibility before God and free access to him. It recognizes the principle of freedom and the principle of individual differences. This means that each individual has not only the right, but the obligation, to discover God in his own experience. This does not rule out the place and importance of the church—the body of Christ—as an aid in securing new insights or as a means of helping the individual clarify, modify, or enrich his own experience. But it does mean that no group—social, ecclesiastical, or otherwise —has the right or power to mediate the grace of God regardless of individual response. Otherwise, Jesus would not have made the break with Judaism, Luther would not have made the break with the Roman Catholic Church, and the free church leaders would not have made their break with the established churches.

This book does not present a systematic treatment of a philosophy of religious education. We have lifted out what seem to be some of the fundamental issues of the Christian faith and have sought to show what these mean for a philosophy and program of religious education. This, then, will be a study of philosophy of religious education in a theological orientation.

Part II

The Nature and Meaning
of the Christian Life

5

Election and the Christian Life

What does it mean to be Christian? When God calls a person to be Christian, what does he call him to be and do? This question is so deep that it cannot be answered fully. It is imperative, however, that the church have as clear an understanding of it as possible, for its answer ultimately gives both content and structure to the "program" of the church.

The task of the church is to seek to lead people to become and to be Christian. If the church is not clear as to what this means, then it is possible for the church through its life and work—its program—to lead people to be something less than that to which God called them. Therefore, in our search for experiential religion and for a philosophy of religious education that will enrich this experiential faith, it is essential that we consider carefully the question: When God calls a person to be Christian, what does he call him to be and do?

Inadequate Views

At the outset let us note some answers that are being given to our question, which, though widely held, are nevertheless inadequate. First, as has been suggested, many people tend to view Christianity in terms of an institutional relationship and institutional loyalty. This loyalty rightly understood and practiced is a thing much to be desired and highly prized. Christians must have institutions in which and through which they engage in worship, study, and service. As a means to an end institutions are not only valuable, they are necessary. But the tendency is present and the pressure is often great to let the institutions become the end. Thus, church members seek to evade the difficult and radical demand of God for total commitment by substituting loyalty to the church as an institution and by merely attending the services and other meetings of the church. Too often when church members do become concerned about their "service" to God, "they are likely to burden themselves with 'church work' instead of 'the work of the church,' being exhausted by activities within the congregation instead of being witnesses as Christians in their daily work."[1]

Sometimes the church itself and we who have promoted the program of the church have contributed to this self-deception on the part of members. Our promotion of the church program is filled with efforts to get people to come to church and attend the meetings. Too often when our people support the church by attending the meetings, they come to feel, perhaps unconsciously, that they thereby have been Christian rather than recognizing that their mission and ministry is in the world and to the world. In attending the services of the church one should discover and receive that which will lead to a total commitment, but sometimes people use church attendance as the substitute for that commitment.

A second inadequate view is the tendency for church members to identify the demands of the Christian life with living up to the accepted social standards of our day. Certainly it is highly desirable that a person live up to the best in the social mores of his community, but too often he does not seek those expressions of the Christian ideals that might lead him above the accepted social standards and would at times lead him contrary to the current mores. Perry is correct when he comments,

The renascence of religion in the West is only an apparent, not an actual, contradiction to rampant secularism and in no way militates against but rather co-operates with secularism's challenge to the Christian faith. Much of the revival in the West is nothing more than the hallowing of "things as they are."[2]

---

[1] Randolph C. Miller, *Christian Nurture and the Church* (New York: Charles Scribner's Sons, 1961), p. 26.

[2] *Op. cit.*, p. 12.

That this criticism of our current expression of the Christian life is justified can hardly be denied. Most of us do not even *know how* to express the ideals of the Christian faith that might take us beyond, or contrary to, the accepted social standards. For example, we urge adults to "be Christian" in their business relations. But what does it mean for one to be Christian in his business relations? Certainly, it means that one should be honest, kind, and courteous. But when we get beyond these rather simple matters, what are the distinctive elements that would make a man truly Christian in his business relations? For most of us, we simply do not know! We are aware that our present social order is not Christian. We are vaguely aware that the standards of Jesus are on a much higher level. We believe, "Thou shalt love thy neighbor as thyself." But just how is this to be expressed in business relations in our present economic order? We do not know! The same holds true for the other areas of our personal and social relationships. We recognize that the Christian life should not be equated with the currently accepted social mores; but because the manner of expressing the Christian ideal is difficult to find, and because expressing it in life is even more difficult, we content ourselves with living up to the present social standards.

There is a third inadequate view. For many people Christianity is viewed primarily in terms of a negative ethic. For these, Christianity is a religion that keeps them from doing certain things. One is known in his Christian life by the things he does not do. Says he, "I don't drink, I don't gamble," and so on. The more devout a person is, the more he doesn't do. "I don't dance, I don't go to the movies on Sunday, I don't wear makeup" and so on into fanaticism.

Of course there are some things a Christian should not do. Disciplining oneself is a part of Christianity—an important part. But this negative ethic does not constitute the heart of Christianity, nor is it the highest expression of Christianity.

The basic fallacy in our thinking at this point is our tendency to identify "not being bad" with "being good." This tendency is seen in many ways. For example, a mother leaves her little boy at home with the oft-repeated admonition, "Johnny, be good while I'm gone." Really, she is not interested in Johnny's being good; she just wants Johnny not to be bad. She wants him not to pull his sister's hair, not to get into a fight with the neighbor's boy, or not to break a window with his baseball. She doesn't care whether he does anything positively good. But not being bad is not the same thing as being good. Not being bad is the absence of a negative quality while being good is the presence of a positive quality.

We might conceive of moral goodness in terms of a scale. One end of the scale we would label "bad" and rate it minus ten. The other end of the scale we would label "good" and rate it plus ten. In the center of the scale would be zero. If a person has been "bad" he would rate on the scale somewhere between minus one and minus ten, depending on the degree of "badness." But if a person has not been bad, he would simply rate at zero. To rate on the "plus" side of the scale one would need to do something positive that was "good."

Let us come back to Johnny. His mother returns and asks, "Have you been good?" He replies, "Yes, Mother." Neither Johnny nor his mother understand what it means to be "good." They both mean, "not been bad." She doesn't mean: has he been kind or helpful, or has he done some positive good? Johnny may have curled up in a chair sound asleep all the time she was gone. If he has not been bad, he just hasn't been bad. It does not at all mean that he has been good.[3]

We need to understand this distinction in terms of our Christianity. It is true that there are things a Christian should not do, but these things do not constitute the highest expression of the Christian life. Christianity is fundamentally a positive religion. In the Sermon on the Mount, Jesus asked the question. "What do ye more than others?" The very question implies its own answer. If you love only those who love you, if you are

---

[3] I am indebted to Professor Ernest M. Ligon for this insight and for the illustration.

friends with only those who are friendly to you, what difference is there between you and the unregenerate? Unregenerate
persons do the same.

In summary Jesus said: "Others say, an eye for an eye, but
I say, turn the other cheek. Others say, love your neighbors and
hate your enemies, but I say, love your enemies." Christians
are to be distinguished by the positive quality of their lives.
The question is, how much are Christians demonstrating this
positive quality of life? We have to confess that as the lives
of Christians are compared with the lives of decently respectable non-Christians in our communities, we find that their lives
are about as good as ours. Perhaps the only difference is that
we go to church and they do not.

We have just been emphasizing the need for a positive
goodness. It must now be said that the primary task of Christianity is not simply to make people "good"; its task is to make
people Christian. This points up a fourth inadequate but widespread view concerning the essential nature and meaning of the
Christian life. Again, let there be no misunderstanding. Of
course Christians must be good. An essential part of the Christian life is high morality, but morality is not all that is involved
in the Christian life. The church errs when it comes to feel
that leading people to live good, clean, moral lives is its ultimate
task. Yet many church leaders are satisfied with this mistaken
view. As a matter of fact, of all the more fundamental objectives
of the Christian life, "being good" is by far the simplest and
easiest to attain. Thus, because church leaders too often do not
know the deeper objectives of the Christian life, and because
these objectives are difficult to achieve, they seem content to
lead church members just to live a good, clean, moral life.

Being "good," as desirable as it is, is not the same thing as
being Christian. An unregenerate person can be "good"; indeed, many of them are. Their honesty, their morality, their
unselfishness, their generosity may be above reproach. Yet, to
be "good" is not necessarily to be Christian. What, then, is the
distinctively Christian aspect of the Christian life? We must

find the answer if we are to know what the church ought to be trying to do.

The Christian Life as Mission and Ministry

It is the contention of the experiential philosophy that the Christian life must be seen and understood in terms of mission and ministry. This is the distinctively Christian aspect of the Christian life. It is to this that God is calling a person when he calls him to be Christian. This view of the Christian life as mission and ministry must be kept in clear focus. When it is in any way blurred, when the Christian life is viewed in lesser terms, the trek toward institutionalism has begun.

The Christian life is certainly related to morality but it is not to be limited to morality. The Christian is expected to be moral, but beyond morality are mission and ministry. For him to accept his mission and to fulfil his ministry in the world is thus the distinctive aspect of the Christian life. Yet our primary efforts at present seem directed toward getting people into the church and to getting them to be moral. We have largely neglected any real sense of mission and ministry *in the world*. Southern Baptist churches have demonstrated real concern to "reach the unreached," to "enlist them for Bible study," and to "win them to Christ." These emphases *we must not lose*. They are entirely worthy as far as they go.

But because we have failed to lead people to understand adequately that the Christian life involves a mission for God in the world, we have built the church as an institution, but the church has not correspondingly increased in its power to minister in and to the world. How else can we explain the fact that today the church is the largest it has ever been in terms of membership, budgets, buildings, and so forth, but at the same time there is more crime, drunkenness, and immorality than ever before?

This evidence of institutionalism in the church is cause for alarm. It will not be enough for us simply to do better what we are already doing. The present situation calls for rather drastic treatment. While morality is fundamental in the Christian life, it is not the primary distinctive of the Christian life needed for our day. Rather, mission and ministry are the distinctives needed for today. To understand clearly this mission and to fulfil this ministry for God in the world is the distinctive demonstration that needs to be given to the world. "As the Father hath sent me, even so send I you" (John 20:21).

So important a matter as the fundamental nature of the Christian life, however, cannot be answered simply on the basis of one passage of Scripture. Rather, the question will have to be answered in light of the total revelation and God's eternal purpose in the world. The God of history is working out his purpose in the world. He has called and is calling unto himself a people, a new Israel, a remnant, through whom his purpose is to be achieved. What is the mission to which he is calling them?

Election and the Life of Israel

Thus, our attention is focused on the doctrine of election. In this doctrine it is clearly set forth that the essence of the life of the new Israel, the remnant, is understood as mission. Election in the Old Testament deals with Israel as a corporate nation and thus cannot be directly related to the individual and his Christian life, but the purpose of election in each is exactly the same. Although there is certainly a distinction to be made between the nation and the individual, these two cannot be compartmentalized as rigidly as some have thought. The nation is always composed of individuals and the individual always exists in community. "Even a passage like the Decalogue, which takes its stand on the level of the election and the covenant and is addressed to the people as a collective whole, expresses its commandments in such a way that their carrying out is possible only by individuals." [4] What light, then,

---

[4] E. Jacob, *Theologie de l'Ancien Testament* (Fr. ed.), pp. 125-126, as quoted in A. Gilmore (ed.), *Christian Baptism* (Philadelphia: The Judson Press, 1959), p. 317, n. 1.

does this doctrine shed upon an understanding of the nature of the Christian life?[5]

The central and fundamental fact to be kept in mind concerning election is that it is never an end within itself. It is always for a purpose, and that purpose is service. Professor Rowley says,

Election is for service. And if God chose Israel, it was not alone that He might reveal Himself to her, but that He might claim her service. Hence Moses mediated the Covenant to Israel, in which she responded in gratitude to the Divine Election and deliverance, and pledged her loyalty to Him who had delivered her—a loyalty as complete and as unconditional as the deliverance had been.[6]

The covenant was first made with Abraham (Gen. 12:1-3). It stated, first, God's eternal purpose: "All the families of the earth are to be blessed," and, second, the means or instrument for accomplishing this purpose, "Thou shalt be a blessing." This covenant was later made with Isaac (Gen. 26:1-4) and with Jacob (Gen. 28:13-15).

The children of Israel did multiply in Egypt, so much so that Egyptian leaders came to fear them as a threat to their national security. The Hebrews were placed in bondage, and their cry of anguish was heard by God. After their mighty deliverance from the hand of Pharaoh, God entered into a covenant relation with the people of Israel.

Now therefore, if ye will obey my voice, indeed, and keep my covenant, then ye shall be a peculiar treasure unto me above all people: for all the earth is mine: and ye shall be unto me a kingdom of priests, and an holy nation. These are the words which thou shalt speak unto the children of Israel. . . . And all the people answered together, and said, All that the Lord hath spoken we will do (Ex. 19:5-6,8).

---

[5] The reader is cautioned not to confuse the doctrine of election with the theological question of predestination; that is, whether one is predestined to salvation or damnation.

[6] H. H. Rowley, *The Biblical Doctrine of Election* (London: Lutterworth Press, 1950), p. 43. Perhaps the best book on this subject, and I gratefully acknowledge my indebtedness to him in this section.

It must be noted that this election was not on the basis of merit. Israel's "high calling to be the Chosen People was not the mark of the Divine indulgence or favouritism, but a summons to a task exacting and unceasing, and election and task were so closely bound together that she could not have the one without the other." [7] C. H. Dodd concurs as he says, "God's choice, however, is (as the prophets are at pains to point out) not an act of favouritism, conferring privileges arbitrarily denied to other peoples. It is election to special responsibility. To be God's chosen people means to be immediately exposed to His Word, with all the momentous consequences that flow from hearing it." [8]

Three factors constitute the essence of Israel's election. First, they were to be recipients of the divine revelation. God was always seeking to reveal himself to man, and Israel was chosen because she was better able to receive that revelation. Second, Israel was to reflect the character of the God who was revealed to her. The standards for the life of man are set by the character of God himself. Third, Israel was to be the instrument to reveal God to man, even to the ends of the earth. They were to be a "kingdom of priests." Their essential function was to be a mediator beween God and man and between man and God. Their mission was to bring man to God. They were to be a channel through whom the knowledge of God was to flow until it covered the earth as the waters cover the sea. Israel accepted this election and promised to fulfil this mission, but she tended to take God as her own exclusive possession and failed to carry out the divine purpose. Ignoring the pleas of the prophets, Israel persisted in her failure.

This last statement calls attention to three additional points that must be understood concerning election. First, response to election is always a voluntary matter. God does not and will not coerce. This covenant relationship is entered on the basis of free choice. Second, this covenant once ratified to fulfil the

---

[7] *Ibid.*, p. 59.
[8] *The Bible To-day* (New York: Cambridge University Press, 1946), p. 107.

purpose of election must be in a state of continuous ratification
by every generation.

It could not be made clearer that here there is no conception of God
being tied to Israel willy-nilly, so that whatever Israel cared to do
He was bound to back her. Her election was not something automatic that made her His people for all time by mere physical generation. She entered into the Covenant voluntarily, and each generation must renew it by accepting for itself its obligations, or it would
place itself outside the Covenant.[9]

Third, election may be repudiated. The covenant which God
made with Israel

offered no right of termination to either party. It declared that God
from His side would never terminate it, but it recognized that Israel
from her side might terminate it, and if she did God would not hold
her to it. By its very nature He could not hold her to it if she wished
to terminate it; for loyalty cannot be compelled. But it is made clear
that if she terminated it, it would not be because by its terms the
Covenant gave her the right to terminate it, but because she dishon-
ourably repudiated it.[10]

"In the fulness of time" Jesus came. His coming was both
redemptive and judgmental for the Jews, as it is for all people.
It is redemptive for those who understand and accept; it is
judgmental for those who refuse. In Matthew 21, Jesus told the
parable of the two sons. One son refused to work in the father's
vineyard but afterward he repented and went. The other son
said he would work in the father's vineyard but he went not.
Here Jesus was trying to help the Jews see their persistent
refusal to fulfil the purpose of their election. His judgment was:
"Verily I say unto you, That the publicans and the harlots go
into the kingdom of God before you" (Matt. 21:31).

Then came the parable of the householder who planted a
vineyard. At harvest time he sent his servants to receive the
fruits of the harvest. But the husbandmen "beat one, and killed
another, and stoned another." Finally, the householder sent his

---

[9] Rowley, *op. cit.*, pp. 47-48.
[10] *Ibid.*, p. 49.

son. Him the husbandmen slew. Then Jesus, the divine Son of God, speaking to the scribes and Pharisees as official representatives of Judaism, made one of the momentous statements in biblical history: "The kingdom of God shall be taken from you, and given to a nation bringing forth the fruits thereof" (Matt. 21:43). Israel had repudiated her election.

But the remnant remains. In the eternal plan and purpose of God the new Israel is now the heir of the election. "But ye are a chosen generation; a royal priesthood, an holy nation, a peculiar people; that ye should shew forth the praises of him who hath called you out of darkness into his marvellous light" (1 Peter 2:9). It is no mere accident that in this passage we find some of the exact phrases that are used in the covenant made with Israel as recorded in Exodus 19:3-6. Those of us who make the claim of being Christian have now entered into this inheritance, this election. We have also entered into this responsibility, this mission.

Election and the Life of the Christian

What does this doctrine teach as we seek to understand the essential nature of the Christian life? As in the case of Israel, our election involves three things. First, we are called by God to receive his revelation. But this calling, this election, is never an end in itself. It is always for a purpose and it demands a dedication on our part to carry out the purpose of this election as complete as the deliverance that has been given to us. Election and mission always go together. We cannot have one without the other. To persist in repudiating the task or in failing to fulfil it is *prima-facie* evidence that one either has not received the revelation or has repudiated the election. In either case the result is the same: the individual is not in a saving relationship with Christ.

Second, we are called to reflect the character of God. This describes the kind and quality of the life of the Christian. The Christian life is demonstrated primarily in terms of positive goodness. Reflecting the character of God in our relations with others, we are to seek to be loving as God is loving, to be for-giving as God is forgiving, to be holy as God is holy.

The third responsibility placed upon us by election is to be instruments of God's redemptive purpose. This is the Christian's mission in the world. This was the task given to Israel in her election; it is the task God gives to the new Israel. When we become one of God's elect, we automatically give ourselves to Jesus to join in his redemptive mission in the world.

As Israel needed desperately to evaluate herself concerning her faithfulness in carrying out this mission, so also do we need to evaluate our faithfulness. How well are we as Christians and as the church fulfilling this responsibility? Statisticians estimate that among Southern Baptists only five out of one hundred ever win a person to Christ. They tell us that in any given year five thousand of our churches do not report a single baptism. They tell us that it takes approximately twenty church mem-bers a whole year to win one person to Christ. In any evangel-istic endeavor our greatest problem is that the church members themselves are not evangelistic. By and large, they leave to the clergy the responsibility for witnessing.

Today the sin of Israel is being repeated. Election continues to be thought of in terms of special privilege rather than in terms of mission. Actually, to be the elect of God, to be Chris-tian, is an awesome thing. It goes beyond our superficial inter-pretation of the Christian life in which a man simply "wants to do better" and "accepts Christ" for the "forgiveness of sin" and in which the church is composed simply of people who want to be "good." Election may be even a dangerous thing. As Rowley says, "the Biblical doctrine of election is therefore penetrated through and through with warning." [11] Jesus de-clared, "Ye have not chosen me, but I have chosen you, and ordained you, that ye should go and bring forth fruit" (John 15:16), and "every branch in me that beareth not fruit he taketh away" (John 15:2). Not to bring forth fruit is a denial of one's election. Thus the exhortation of Holy Writ is to be

[11] *Ibid.*, p. 168.

taken with utmost seriousness: "Brethren, give diligence to make your calling and election sure" (2 Peter 1:10).

Some clear thinking needs to be done at this point. As the church leads an individual to "accept Christ" and become Christian, it must make clear to the potential convert the mission to which God is calling him. If he is confused about the nature of the life to which he has been called, and if he responds with something less than full commitment, then he may also be confused about his relationship to God. Precisely at this point the Pharisees erred. They said, "Abraham is our father." Jesus replied, "If ye were Abraham's children, ye would do the works of Abraham" (John 8:39). Israel thought she was the heir of the promises of God, but she deceived herself concerning the nature of the promise and the election. Paul said, "For he is not a Jew, which is one outwardly; neither is that circumcision, which is outward in the flesh: but he is a Jew, which is one inwardly" (Rom. 2:28-29). Or again, "For they are not all Israel, which are of Israel: neither, because they are the seed of Abraham, are they all children" (Rom. 9:6-7).

So we, too, may deceive ourselves. Having inherited a traditional interpretation of the nature of the Christian life and having followed a pattern of the Christian life that falls far short of the New Testament demands, we may be as surprised as the Pharisees at the judgment of God.

It cannot be too strongly emphasized that if the Church is the heir of the election of Israel she is also the heir of the warnings that her heritage is cast away if she is not loyal to the purpose of that election. Her election is conditional on her desiring to retain it, and that can only be tested by her desire to fulfil its obligations. . . . And when a Church turns in on itself and becomes a mutual improvement society, and regards itself as a little Ark of safety in a troubled world, instead of charged with a mission to the world, it turns its back on its election.[12]

The individual and the church who have been called by God to receive his revelation and who have been elected to be in-

---

[12] *Ibid.*, pp. 166, 174.

struments of his redemptive purpose still stand under the judgment of God for their faithfulness in carrying out the purpose of their election.

Is Growth in the Christian Life Optional?

A major question which has been implicit in the previous section but now needs to be dealt with directly is this: Is growth in the Christian life optional? Is development toward and in the mission for which one is saved optional? We seek to lead people to "accept Christ as Saviour." After an individual has done this, we urge him to grow in the Christian life. This practice in our churches give the impression that whether the new convert grows or not is optional with him. Many evidently choose not to grow.

However, growing in the Christian life, training for service, developing in the Christian life to be effective instruments for witnessing these are not optional for the Christian.

They inhere in the conversion experience and in the nature of the Christian life to which the convert has been called. Hodge was right when he said, "Any man who thinks he is a Christian, and that he has accepted Christ for justification, when he did not at the same time accept him for sanctification, is miserably deluded in that very experience." [13] Those who contemplate becoming a Christian and those who become Christian need to understand that conversion is not accepting a set of beliefs, it is not a transaction. It is entering into a relationship with God. It is a new birth into a new way of life. In this new life, by virtue of a new relationship with God, one surrenders himself to be an instrument of God.

Now, whether one will be an instrument or not, or whether one will develop himself to be an instrument, is not optional. Physical illustrations used to explain spiritual relationships are always inadequate but they might be suggestive. A branch may be grafted into the trunk of a tree. If the branch and the trunk

---

[13] A. A. Hodge as quoted in A. H. Strong, *Systematic Theology* (Philadelphia: Judson Press, 1907), p. 869.

enter into a vital relationship, that is, if they unite so that life flows from the trunk into the branch, the branch will grow. Growth is evidence that a vital union has taken place. Failure to grow is evidence that a vital union has not taken place.

Therefore, the problem of unenlisted, undeveloped, and untrained members, which plagues most of our churches, stems from a basic misunderstanding of the nature of the Christian life. The problem is of the church's own making because it probably failed to lead the potential convert and the prospective member to face the real demands of the Christian life. For a church to have to "beg" its members to train for service and to fulfil their ministry in the world is inconsistent with the essential nature and meaning of the Christian life. Growth, training, and development in the Christian life are not highly desirable additions to the new birth—they are of the essence of the "new birth" kind of life. Growth is not optional for one who is *in Christ!*

This is one reason for a church considering the advisability of having a "period of waiting" between a person's profession of faith and his reception into full church membership.[14] It would afford the church an opportunity to see whether the individual was giving evidence in his life of a deepening awareness of his mission and a real commitment to the ministry to which he had been called in making his profession of faith. Also, this period of waiting would convince the convert that the church expected such growth.

To suggest that growth in the Christian life is essential does not mean to imply that this growth is automatic. It simply means that when one enters into a *saving* relationship with Christ, the very nature of the relationship involves growth. He has the choice of whether he will surrender his life to Christ as Saviour and Lord, but once this surrender is made, he has submitted to a relationship in which growth in understanding of and commitment to the mission for which he was saved is essential.

---

[14] Discussed in chapter 11.

Thus the individual who does not grow because he deliberately refuses to do so, simply gives evidence that he is not "in Christ" because the "in Christ" relationship is a *growing relationship* (Mark 4:3-9; John 15:1-8).

Those who disagree with this view might cite the passage in 1 Corinthians 3:12-15, which reads in part, "Now if any man build upon this foundation gold, silver, precious stones, wood, hay, stubble; every man's work shall be made manifest. . . . If any man's work shall be burned, he shall suffer loss: but he himself shall be saved; yet so as by fire." It is quite clear, however, that this passage does not refer to the quality of one's life but rather to the quality of one's ministry; it refers to teachers rather than to converts.

Here . . . the reference is to a testing, not of the converts, but of the work of the teachers. . . . It is possible for a teacher of good or exemplary character to be guilty of poor workmanship. The latter will be destroyed, but the teacher will be saved despite the destruction of his work.[15]

Lange concurs: "To suppose . . . that there is any allusion to the private work of personal sanctification, would be untenable, inasmuch as the entire context treats solely of ministerial functions." [16] Finally, there is the statement by Archibald Robertson and Alfred Plummer:

The various kinds of superstructure represent various degrees of inferiority in the *ministry* of the "afterbuilders," *i.e.*, according as they make, or fail to make, a lasting contribution to the structure. . . . The Apostle does not mean that every teacher who takes Christ as the basis of his teaching will necessarily be saved: his meaning is that a very faulty teacher may be saved, and "will be saved, if at all, so as through fire."[17]

---

[15] *The Interpreter's Bible* (New York: Abingdon Press, 1953), X, 48-49.

[16] John Peter Lange, *Lange's Commentary on the Holy Scriptures* (Grand Rapids: Zondervan Publishing House, 1956), p. 76.

[17] A. T. Robertson and Alfred Plummer, *A Critical and Exegetical Commentary on the First Epistle of St. Paul to the Corinthians* (*The International Critical Commentary* [Edinburgh: T. & T. Clark, 1911]), pp. 62, 65.

This passage, therefore, rather than being in opposition to, is strong support for the basic thesis of this book. It speaks directly to our situation. Ministers and other staff members may be exceedingly busy about the work of the church; they may work hard and sincerely, but if they are building with inferior material (work that does not come up to the true standard of God and, therefore, will not stand the test), the individual, himself, will be saved but his work will go for naught. The work that is sound survives; that which is erroneous is consumed.

6

The Priesthood of Believers
and the Christian Life

We turn now to another doctrine in our search for an answer to the nature of the life to which God is calling man. If the doctrine of election teaches that Christians, the people of God, have a mission in the world and points with unmistakable clarity to what that mission is, the doctrine of the priesthood of believers teaches with equal clarity that Christians have a ministry and indicates where and how this ministry is to be performed. Dr. Kenneth E. Kirk, the bishop of Oxford, points to the centrality of this doctrine by saying that the priesthood of all believers is "the decisive formula of all non-episcopal Christendom."[1] Yet this doctrine, which Baptists have claimed as a distinctive principle, has, unfortunately, been largely misunderstood and inadequately expressed. In breaking with the sacramental and ecclesiastical view of the church, Baptists have usually interpreted this doctrine to mean only that every believer has free and direct access to God without the necessity of a priest as mediator. While this interpretation is certainly true, it is only half the meaning of this doctrine. What Baptists and others of the free church tradition have failed to understand adequately is that the priesthood of believers also teaches that every Christian is a priest or minister and thus has a ministry to perform. As Trueblood has pointed out,

Most Protestants pay lip service to the Reformation doctrine of the priesthood of every believer, but they do not thereby mean to say that every Christian is a minister. Many hasten to add that all they

---

[1] Kenneth E. Kirk (ed.), *The Apostolic Ministry* (London: Hodder & Stoughton, Ltd., 1946), p. 48.

mean by the familiar doctrine is that nobody needs to confess to a priest, since each can confess directly to God. The notion that this doctrine erases the distinction between laymen and minister is seldom presented seriously, and would, to some, be shocking, but it does not take much study of the New Testament to realize that the early Christians actually operated on this revolutionary basis.[2]

Some scholars feel that the priesthood of believers can be interpreted only in a collective sense. Others argue that this doctrine has both individual and corporate aspects. "The priesthood of believers means each believer offering his own body: it also means Christ the high-priest offering his body, the Church. These two aspects of the one perpetual offering may be distinguished in thought: they cannot be separated in fact."[3] For our purpose this distinction is not of primary importance; for whether it is viewed individually or collectively, the essential purpose is always the same—ministry.

In spite of the importance that has been attached to this doctrine since the Reformation, and in spite of the fact that it is one of the distinctives in the free church tradition, there is a dearth of material written on this subject. Fortunately, there is a growing interest at the present time. Yet, as late as 1958 Hendrik Kraemer was able to say, "A systematic attempt at a theological foundation and motivation of the laity's place and meaning, as inherent in the nature and calling of the Church, has not so far been undertaken."[4] Such a theological foundation is imperative. After pointing out that lay movements are beginning to spring up on the Continent, in England, and in the United States, he says,

---

[2] *Op. cit.*, p. 30.

[3] T. W. Manson, *Ministry and Priesthood: Christ's and Ours* (London: The Epworth Press, 1959), p. 64. Torrance disagrees. He sees the priesthood of believers only in a collective sense. "The expression 'priesthood of all believers' is an unfortunate one as it carries with it a ruinous individualism. 'Priest' in the singular is never found in the New Testament applied to the believer, any more than 'king' in the singular. In the singular these words could only apply to Christ himself. Like the term 'saints' used only collectively in the New Testament, 'priests' and 'kings' apply corporately to the whole membership of the church." T. F. Torrance, *Royal Priesthood* (London: Oliver & Boyd, Ltd., 1955), p. 35, n. 1.

[3] *Op. cit.*, p. 30.

All this new activity, . . . which in so many respects evokes much gratitude and joy, will ultimately fail if it has no lasting and serious theological foundation. It will appear in the future mere temporary effervescence or a passing eruption of activism, without real backbone, if it is not undergirded by a well-thought-out theology of the laity on a biblical basis.[5]

Fresh emphasis on this doctrine means that our deeper and clearer understanding of the nature of the Christian life must find its roots in nothing less than the eternal purpose of God. It means that the laity of our churches must come to understand that the Christian life is a ministry, and this ministry is performed in response to the call of God and under the judgment of God. The issue for our churches is not that here is a vast, untapped source of man power that needs to be captured and put to work; the issue is that the churches must come to know what is God's design for the laity in his eternal purpose. It is this that gives the direction to the layman's ministry. *No program of promotion can take the place of this basic biblical understanding.*

The Teaching of the New Testament

What, then, is the New Testament view of the ministry of the laity that will provide this theological foundation? Only a brief sketch is possible here. The most direct references to the priesthood of believers are found in 1 Peter and Revelation. Revelation 1:5-6 refers to Christ who, "hath made us kings and priests unto God." The "new song" in praise to Christ mentions Christians as "kings and priests" (Rev. 5:10). Revelation 20:6 predicts that Christians "shall be priests of God and of Christ." In 1 Peter, Christians are called "an holy priesthood" whose function it is "to offer up spiritual sacrifices" (2:5). They are a "royal priesthood" whose task is to praise him who had called them "out of darkness into his marvellous light" (2:9).

What kind of sacrifices were they to offer? Finding the true answer is important because the nature of the sacrifices will

---

[5] *Ibid.,* pp. 13-14.

determine the nature of this ministry of the laity. A part of the answer is found in Hebrews where the uniqueness of the sacrifice of Jesus, the great High Priest, is magnified. "His sacrifice is defined as the doing of God's will. It was his body that God desired, not sacrifices and offerings." [6] What, then, is the nature of the sacrifice of the priesthood of believers? They are to offer themselves. They are to present their "bodies a living sacrifice" (Rom. 12:1) to be instruments of redemption as they "show forth the praises of him" who had called them "out of darkness into his marvellous light." Thus when one unites with the community of believers, when one enters into the priesthood of believers, he is thereby uniting with Jesus in God's redemptive purpose in the world. Any program of religious education that does not make this clear is failing at a fundamental point.

Throughout the New Testament one finds this emphasis on the ministry of the laity. Paul's letters were addressed to the churches, to all the members, not just to the leaders. He reminded them of their "holy calling" and their "ministry."

And all things are of God, who hath reconciled us to himself by Jesus Christ, and hath given to us the ministry of reconciliation; to wit, that God was in Christ, reconciling the world unto himself, not imputing their trespasses unto them; and hath committed unto us the word of reconciliation (2 Cor. 5:18-19).

Robinson points out that "the New Testament is full of expressions referring to 'calling,' 'being called,' 'to be called,' and they always refer to *all* Christians and not to what we style 'ministers.' All Christians are ministers, 'called' to a ministry."[7]

It is true that both *kleros* (clergy) and *laos* (laity) appear in the New Testament, "but, strange to say, they denote the same people, not different peoples." [8] For example, in 2 Corinthians 6:16 we find, "For ye are the temple of the living God;

---

[6] Paul S. Minear, *Images of the Church in the New Testament* (Philadelphia: The Westminster Press, 1960), p. 100.

[7] William Robinson, *Completing the Reformation* (Lexington, Ky.: The College of the Bible, 1955), pp. 19-20.

[8] *Ibid.*, p. 17.

as God hath said, I will dwell in them, and walk in them; and I will be their God, and they shall be my people [laos]." While in 1 Peter 5:3 we find the writer exhorting the elders not to view themselves as being "lords over your charges [kleroi], but being ensamples to the flock."

This, of course, is not to suggest that there was not some type of "official ministry" in the New Testament. In the passage just cited the elders would be viewed as the "official ministry." Yet they were warned about the danger of making too wide a distinction between themselves and their charges (kleroi) so that they would tend to "lord it over" them.

In Ephesians 4 we have the most mature statement in the New Testament concerning the "official ministry." Here Paul spoke of apostles, prophets, evangelists, and pastors and teachers (v. 11). He then described their work as being "for the perfecting of the saints, for the work of the ministry, for the edifying of the body of Christ" (v. 12). In this connection, Robinson has a very interesting suggestion: "The comma after 'saints' is not in the Greek text and I would contend that it ought not to be there at all. Then the official ministers' chief job is to equip the saints for the work of the ministry." [9]

In light of the doctrine of the priesthood of believers it would seem that the integrating principle around which the pastor's ministry is to be built is: "equip the saints for the work of the ministry." At the present time the minister is pulled asunder by the overwhelming and sometimes conflicting demands made upon him. He is to preach. He is to evangelize. He is to engage in social action. He is to administer. He is to visit. He is to counsel. For him to attempt to do all these alone is impossible from the human perspective and erroneous from the biblical perspective. Committed to the priesthood of believers, he should evaluate each of the multitudinous demands made upon him by asking: Does this activity contribute to my efforts to "equip the saints for the work of the ministry" or does it interfere with this effort? It is the task of the minister to equip

---

[9] *Ibid.*, p. 21.

the "saints" to witness, counsel, administer, teach, engage in social action, and so on.

Also by this principle can we evaluate the effectiveness of the church's program. Is the curriculum designed to give *specific* training in equipping the saints for the work of the ministry? If not, it ought to be changed. Are the activities of teaching and training in the various organizations of the church *actually* equipping the saints for the work of the ministry, and are the people actually engaging in this ministry in the world? If not, the work of these organizations needs to be modified to achieve this fundamental objective.

In the New Testament community there was no office that corresponded to the Jewish concept of priest. "The only priests under the Gospel, designated as such in the New Testament, are the saints, the members of the Christian brotherhood." [10] T. W. Manson points out that when priests were converted (Acts 6:7), they did not thereby perform the function of priest (in the Jewish sense) in the Christian community. Since the listing of the church ministries in 1 Corinthians 12:28-30 and Ephesians 4:11-12 does not mention priests, Manson concludes that in the New Testament church "there was not room for a regular priesthood, *as priesthood was understood in that time.*" [11] However, the tendency toward institutionalism in this area is recognized, for he says that by the end of the second century the office of bishop had become "a sacrificial office, as was that of the Jewish priests." He goes on to say,

The fact is that there is here a parting of the ways: priesthood is on the way to be completely bound up with the right of a specialized group within the Church to offer the eucharistic sacrifice of bread and cup identified with the body and blood of Christ. The priesthood of all believers, on the other hand, is on the way to become a godly sentiment with little or no relevance to the day-to-day practice of the Church at worship.[12]

[10] J. B. Lightfoot, *The Christian Ministry* (London: Macmillan & Co., Ltd., 1901), p. 6.
[11] *Op. cit.*, p. 44.
[12] *Ibid.*, p. 68.

Recapturing the Ministry of the Laity

One of the major attacks of the Reformation was centered at the point of recapturing the ministry of the laity. Yet, strange to say, this was one of the areas where a sufficiently radical break was not made by the reformers and those who followed them. The modern church can make here a significant and unique contribution if it will dare to do so. Trueblood points out that one of the central characteristics of the Reformation was in opening the Bible to the "ordinary Christian," and then he says,

Now, after more than three centuries, we can, if we will, change gears again. Our opportunity *for a big step lies in opening the ministry to the ordinary Christian in much the same manner that our ancestors opened Bible reading to the ordinary Christian.* To do this means, in one sense, the inauguration of a new Reformation while in another it means the logical completion of the earlier Reformation in which the implications of the position taken were neither fully understood nor loyally followed.[13]

In the churches today the laity in the main has the attitude that the primary responsibility for ministry rests in the hands of the clergy. The layman feels that he should "support" the ministry and the church with his money, by attending the services, and by doing some work, primarily for and in the church. Still the layman feels that the major responsibility for carrying out the ministry of God in the world rests with the clergy. This is exactly the pattern followed by the three religious movements considered earlier in their trek toward institutionalism. The rather sharp distinction that exists today in the churches between the clergy and the laity finds no basis in the New Testament.

For the modern church to recapture the New Testament emphasis on the ministry of the laity "would mean no less than a revolution in the conception of the Church, in its relation to its members and in its relation to the outside world, if it

---

[13] *Op. cit.*, p. 32.

were realized in its full consequences." [14] Revolutionary though it may be, recapture it we must. This is not simply a desirable doctrine, *this is the key by which Christians are to accomplish their mission in the world as the people of God!*

Yet, to recapture this emphasis on the ministry of the laity will be exceedingly difficult. For example, in our day the attitude has become dominant that being a Christian makes relatively few demands on a person. We have come to think of the Christian life in terms of petty moral requirements and institutional relationships. Thus, this mind set almost guarantees that the average church member (and perhaps the average preacher and church vocational worker) will find it exceedingly difficult to comprehend the deep demands of God concerning the Christian life—demands in terms of mission and ministry—when these are presented to him. When a minister in the pulpit invites people to "make a decision for Christ," usually it is not this "ministry" to which he is inviting people. When people respond with a "decision," it is generally not this "ministry" to which they commit their lives. Yet, the experiential philosophy holds that this is the very essence of the Christian life!

Does this mean that we must modify significantly our invitation to people for Christian discipleship? Does it mean that we may need a period of waiting before receiving people into church membership so that they will have opportunity to give evidence that they understand and accept this ministry? These questions suggest the revolutionary implications which this emphasis might have for any church that dares to take it seriously.

A Ministry in the World

The primary ministry of the laity must be performed in the world. This does not mean that the church services and life would be neglected. It does mean that the doctrine of the priesthood of believers "implies a relation of the church to

---

[14] H. H. Walz, "Adult Christianity," *The Shane Quarterly*, XV, 1954, p. 187.

the world which is of the utmost significance." [15] Obscuring
this relationship has blunted the attack of the church, for the
laity is the spearhead of the church in the world. This was
true in the New Testament when "they that were scattered
abroad went every where preaching the word" (Acts 8:4). It
was also true in the next three centuries:

The first prominent theological thinkers on behalf of the Church,
were laymen of great ability. To mention only a few of the very
prominent: Tertullian, Cyprian, Augustine. Cyprian and Augustine,
having become bishops so to speak by surprise, were essentially, by
their whole education and long "secular career," laymen. The reason
why such an obvious fact has to be stated expressly is that their
position as Church Fathers has put them so forcefully in the theological, i.e. non-lay, category that the simple truth of their being
thinking Christian laymen is entirely forgotten or ignored. [16]

The New Testament term "laity" and the modern term "layman" are quite different in meaning. In modern terminology
a "layman" is one who is a nonprofessional in a particular
vocation. That is, a "layman" in medicine means one who is
untrained in medicine. The implication is always present that
the professional is the one who has the primary responsibility
for doing the work. This is not the case in religion nor in the
teaching of the New Testament. Nowhere does the New Testament say that the primary responsibility for accomplishing
the purpose of God in the world rests in the hands of the
"official ministry." The primary responsibility is always upon
the shoulders of those "called to be saints" the *laos theou,*
"the people of God." Thus in religion it is the layman who
must do most of the work in the world.

This is true first of all because, as has been pointed out, it
is the teaching of Scripture. In the second place it is true because it is in the world that the ministry of the Christian can
best be expressed. The world is where he works; that is where

[15] E. G. Selwyn (ed.), *The First Epistle of St. Peter* (London: Macmillan
& Co., Ltd., 1946), p. 292.
[16] Kraemer, *op. cit.,* pp. 20-21.

most of his time is spent. Therefore, the layman must have primary responsibility for giving the witness of God in the world. Third, because he is only one person, the minister is limited in the number of places he can be in the world. Witness must be given in the shop, in the service station, in the home, in the office, on the farm. It is humanly impossible for the minister to be in all these places. But there are Christian laymen in these places. Therefore, contrary to prevailing opinion, it is the laymen and not the clergy who have the primary responsibility to do most of the work in the world. This is not meant to minimize nor excuse the clergy; it is simply an attempt to get the laity in proper perspective.

In the fourth place it is in the world where the witness for God is most desperately needed. "It is the universality of human sin and corruption which makes it necessary that there should be in the midst of the world a priestly body which can 'stand on the Godward side' on behalf of men." [17] This is where the people are. Even with the best programs of enlistment and the most effective approaches to mass evangelism yet devised, the church has been able to reach only a relatively small percentage of the total population of any community (particularly in large urban centers) with anything like a continuing ministry. Increasingly the church is ministering to "its own" while the masses are left untouched by what goes on within the walls of the church. In this connection the observation of Walz concerning the "gathered church" is most provocative:

I have often wondered in recent years whether it has not been a mistake to concentrate the doctrine of the Church so much on its being gathered. I think that the Church will appear to be gathered from the four winds of the earth only at the end of history as we know it. For the time being the Church is not a gathered community, but, to use the paradoxical phrase of one of the Reformers (Melanchthon), "the community of the dispersed." Without dispersion there is no savour. It is the laymen, not gathered in the church

---

[17] Selwyn, *op. cit.*, p. 293.

building, but busy everywhere in the world, who must truly represent the Church as an element of stimulation, of creativeness and
criticism, as a challenge demanding response which means *life* for
the world.[18]

The doctrine of the priesthood of believers is closely related
to the Christian doctrine of vocation, which means that the
totality of one's life is to be lived under God and for God. This
ministry for God in the world means that the totality of the
Christian life is bound up in Christ. His work and his play must
be "in Christ." It means that how he earns and spends his
money is just as sacred an obligation and just as spiritual a
ministry as the tithe he gives to the church. The witness he
gives as he makes his living is as important as the witness he
gives on Sunday.

When a church is not making satisfactory progress, the membership usually feels that it needs to change preachers. Sometimes what is needed is a radical change in the congregation.
The "Word" must become flesh in the minister, but it must also
become flesh in the congregation. It must be clothed by the
lives of the congregation if it is to be taken to the slums, the
stores, the office, to the world standing in desperate need of the
"word" from God. Talking about "love for God" may be pious
mouthing unless the congregation expresses that love beyond
the church into work, community, and world.

Two major barriers tend to stand between the modern organized church and the world in which it is set. One is sociological
and one is psychological. From the sociological perspective our
churches are coming increasingly to be identified with the middle-class, white-collar attitudes, standards, and values. There
are exceptions, of course. But in the main the lowest economic
group is largely untouched. The few who are being reached are
being reached by religious groups labeled "sects." Also, the
church in general has lost almost completely the labor union
man. In many places the labor unions now have their union
meetings at eleven o'clock on Sunday morning. Likewise, the

---

[16] *Op. cit.,* p. 103.

chief executives and the wealthy managers are by and large
unreached. The church must break out of the middle-class,
white-collar shackles in its concern for the ministry to all people
of all classes.

The psychological barrier is related to the "official ministry."
When the preachers speak, when they visit, when they witness,
there is always the conscious or unconscious awareness on the
part of the recipient that "they are paid to do it." Their ministry
undoubtedly is fruitful, but its effectiveness is limited by this
very real difficulty.

The solution to both these problems can be found in the ministry of the laity in the world. The only way to overcome these
difficulties

is to decentralize the life of the church. . . . If . . . we force Christian
people to engage their Christian "capital" in living together with
those outside the church, e.g. their colleagues at work, their part-
ners in business, their political friends, their fellow members in professional associations, instead of clinging together with their Christian brothers five evenings a week, we shall not only help them to be
witnesses of the Gospel to those who do not know it, but also to
overcome for themselves the peculiar atmosphere prevailing in the
church and to be Christians breathing the air of modern life.[19]

Two questions remain to be faced. How well is the church
fulfilling its ministry in the world, and how well qualified is
the laity for carrying out their ministry? On the first question
there would undoubtedly be overwhelming agreement that the
modern church is not in any adequate measure "in the world"
through its laity in those spheres of the world (factories, shops,
schools, government agencies, labor unions, etc.) where the
real issues of the faith are being fought today.

The field is not the church, but the *world*. . . . There are practical
overtones for this truth in the deadly struggle of Christianity with
Communism. Communism got its start and derives its strength from
a ghetto Christianity. When Karl Marx said that religion was the
opiate of the people, he meant that religion, by wrapping men's

---

[19] Walz, *op. cit.*, p. 189.

minds in the mists of other worldliness, insulated men from the struggles and problems of our common life together in the world. When people say, "Let religion stay out of politics," "Let religion stay out of business," "Let religion stay out of everything but a little narrow corner of things which we will gladly assign to it"—when people say such things, they are giving voice to the Communist interpretation of the function of religion in society. To constrict the function of the Christian faith in the world in this fashion would fatally wound our witness and falsify the mission which we have been given.[20]

Yet, unfortunately, this is what is happening in the modern church. Some say the church should be concerned only with "spiritual" matters, that the church is to be concerned only with man's relation to God. Man's religion is to be expressed primarily in the church. The more dedicated ones will assume some leadership responsibility in the church. In the world he is expected, of course, to be "good." But the fact that the Christian has a ministry which must be performed in the world as a fundamental expression of his faith is almost completely foreign to the understanding of the average church member.

On the second question many feel that the average church member is both spiritually illiterate and powerless in giving his Christian witness where most of his life is spent. Therefore, in the program of our churches there must be far more specific emphasis, in teaching and in practice, on the ministry of the laity in the world. The curriculum must be designed with this emphasis in clear focus. Every Christian has a ministry which, under God, he must fulfil. He cannot pay someone else to do it either by buying indulgences or by tithing. Therefore, every person who commits himself to Christ should understand that in entering the Christian fellowship he thereby is covenanting with God to accept and fulfil this ministry. He ought to understand and accept this responsibility *before* he unites with the church.

If the emphasis of this chapter is correct, then the program

[20] Culbert G. Rutenber, *The Reconciling Gospel* (Philadelphia: The Judson Press, 1960), p. 114.

of the modern churches is going in the wrong direction. That is, almost everything that churches plan and prepare for points toward what is to be done *on Sunday in the church.* The minister and church staff make their plans, a visitation program is promoted, the teachers and other church leaders make their preparation—all pointing to Sunday as the climax. All of this is good as far as it goes. Certainly worship and Bible study are basic, but the priesthood of believers points to a *climax* in Christian work and witness in what is done *in the world during the week!* What happens on Sunday is to prepare the believer for that ministry.

Of course, this is what the present church program intends to do, but a significant revolution will be needed if this concept is seriously undertaken in the life and work of the churches. The present mind set and attitude of the pastors and church staff members will have to be drastically changed. The "success" and effectiveness of their work must be measured not by how many "attended" on Sunday but by what those do in the world who attend on Sunday. Church members also will have to change their understanding of their responsibility for, relation to, and ministry in the world. These are some of the changes that must be made if the modern churches are to implement the practical meaning of the New Testament doctrine of the priesthood of believers.

But to have a deeper understanding of their ministry is not enough. They must also have training for this ministry. To provide this training in any adequate sense will call for a new curriculum. Christians will need the opportunity to study specifically and in depth their relationships in the world. The factory worker should have the stimulation and the opportunity to study what his ministry is in the world and how it should be expressed in normal relationships—in the home, in society, in the factory. The doctor, the accountant, the lawyer, the farmer, the secretary—all should be provided the same opportunity.

This is not to suggest that one's ministry in the world will be expressed only through his particular vocation. Often a Christian's ministry will be expressed quite apart from his vocation. At a given time he might be concerned with the problem of juvenile delinquency, or he might give himself to an intensive effort to reach the unreached through visitation. Again, he might desire to give special study and work for the world mission task of the church, or he might give himself to the elimination of injustice in some area of society.

Therefore, the objective of the church and the emphasis of its program must be changed to whatever degree is necessary to help the membership understand the essential mission God has entrusted to those whom he has called to be the people of God, and to lead them to accept and fulfil this ministry *in the world.*

7

The Will of God and
the Christian Life

Our search continues for an answer to the question: What does it mean to be a Christian? Unregenerate people can be moral, kind, thoughtful, and unselfish. Thus, while these are important aspects of the Christian life, they are not the essential distinctives. What is it a Christian must be and do which no unregenerate person can be and do? Jesus declared that a tree is known by its fruit. "A good tree cannot bring forth evil fruit, neither can a corrupt tree bring forth good fruit. . . . Wherefore by their fruits ye shall know them" (Matt. 7:18-20). But what is the nature of this "fruit"? Jesus gave a clear answer: Fruit comes in doing "the will of my Father which is in heaven" (v. 21).

Thus, if the essential nature of the Christian life is to be understood in terms of mission and ministry, the concept of "the will of God" provides the framework in which this mission and ministry are to be accomplished. Speaking of the individual's responsibility before God for the life he lives, Niebuhr said, "The will of God is the norm . . . and the individual faces the awful responsibility of seeking to do God's will amidst all the complexities of human existence with no other authoritative norm but that ultimate one." [1] Jesus' statement, "Not my will but thine be done," was not resignation to the inevitable. It was not simply a passive acceptance of an undesirable experience. Rather, this statement meant, "I am determined that thy will shall be done even if it means death for me." Here

---

[1] Reinhold Niebuhr, *The Nature and Destiny of Man* (New York: Charles Scribner's Sons, 1941), I, 60.

is a positive determination that the will of God shall be done—at any cost.

What, then, does it mean for a person to be Christian? It means that a person has come into such a relationship of love, faith, surrender, and commitment to God through Christ that with Jesus he can say, "Thy will be done," with a positive determination that the will of God shall be done—and will be done through him—whatever the cost. This is something no unregenerate person can do, no matter how "good" he may be.

To do the will of God, then, is the distinctively Christian aspect of the Christian life, but it must be done in God's name and for God's glory. An unregenerate social reformer may engage in causes that parallel the will of God, but this is done for his own sake or for humanitarian reasons. Fine as this is, it is not action "in Christ" or "unto God." The will of God must be done "unto God" and as a person's witness to God.

What Is the Will of God?

Thus, being Christian means that one has joined with Jesus in the positive determination to do the will of God whatever the cost to him personally. Here we come face to face with the radical demand in the Christian life which has been inadequately understood and certainly inadequately expressed by the modern church member. What is the nature of this radical demand and how is it to be expressed today? To find the answer the Christian simply asks, "What is the will of God that I am to do?"

The answer to this question is to be found in the total revelation of God. The experiential philosophy contends that the search for the answer to this question must become the fundamental quest of the church. The people whom God has called to be Christian, who in faith have responded to his call, must ask themselves questions such as: What is the will of God for the world? What is the will of God that should be done in my community? What is the will of God that should be done in this political situation? What is the will of God that should be done in this slum situation? What is the will of God that should be done in business relations, in home relations, indeed, in all relations?

Although these are significant questions in practicing the Christian life, they are questions for which the modern church has no adequate answers. While winning the lost is a major responsibility of Christians (to be emphasized in the next chapter), there are also other things in the will of God that need to be done. If a pastor wants to take this seriously and asks his congregation, "What can we do in our community to achieve the will of God?" can he, and can they, give an adequate answer to this question? If they cannot, it is a judgment upon them. In the church Christians are taught, "Do unto others as you would have them do unto you," "Blessed are the peacemakers," "Go the second mile with Christ." But, specifically, how do Christians give expression to these teachings in their human and social relations?

Herein is a basic part of the problem. The preaching and the teaching that has been done in the churches have led people to accept Christianity in terms of such generalized ideals that almost anyone can agree with them. But these people have not known how these generalized ideals are to be implemented and expressed in specific situations.[2] This emphasis does not mean that Christianity is to be made a series of petty *do's and don't's*. It simply means that Christians are seriously to seek to know the will of God in the world so they can work within it in specific situations.

The major tragedy is not that we do not know the answers to these questions, for they are exceedingly complex and difficult. *The real tragedy is that these are questions which most churches are not even asking!* Nor do they seem to be seeking answers. Rather, too often our churches deal with safe issues in a superficial manner.

Perhaps these questions are not being asked because of

the haunting suspicion that the answers might lead to a cross
—even as they did for Jesus. It is no wonder that the church
is being ignored by the world. The church is not a creative fountain where "ideas flourish and thought patterns are
formed." The church has lost the distinctive and radical
demands of the New Testament and, too often, it is guilty
of simply trying to put the religious stamp on things as they
are.

How to Find the Will of God

The will of God will be sought through study groups—small
and large—on the local church level, on the denominational
level, and on the worldwide level. In the local church this
study may well be done within the present organizational
structure where interested and involved people will study a
particular problem specifically and in depth—certainly for more
than one Sunday!

In a recent political campaign in a large Southern city, a
leading candidate for a major office said that "if he were a
businessman, his firm's racial policies would be determined
by the effects of integration on profits." He also said that
he thought "most businessmen decide their racial practices
according to the probable effect on profits." [3] It is quite probable that many businessmen in our churches make some
fundamental decisions on just this basis. This is the kind of
problem that ought to be given specific attention by small
study groups. Is this the kind of witness the Christian businessman should give in the world? Is profit the only or even
the major motive for the Christian? What fundamental Christian principles should guide his decisions? Surely, this would
be a matter of great importance for a Christian who is *genuinely* seeking to find and to follow the will of God.

This assumes that the church member has come into such
a personal and unique relationship with Jesus Christ that he

---

[3] *The Louisville Times,* October 23, 1961, p. 1.

genuinely wants to know the will of God in order that he may express it in the world as his witness to God. Of course, the layman will participate in the visitation and witnessing efforts of his church as they engage in "outreach for the unreached." He will also participate in the organized life of his church by accepting leadership responsibilities. But important as these are, they do not constitute his fundamental ministry in the world nor his highest witness. Rather, his primary ministry will be demonstrated as he discovers and expresses in his relationships in the world those courses of action which, in the will of God, go beyond the current demands of society or contrary to the current mores. There can be no greater witness than this! This was the kind of witness given by the Christians of the first century. This is the witness of experiential religion. No program of visitation, regardless of how effective it may be, can take the place of this kind of witnessing in the world. Nor can any program of visitation be as effective as this kind of witnessing.

The opponents of this view are constantly reminding us of the difficulty and complexity of our ethical problems: Is it wrong to drink intoxicating liquors in moderation? Is it wrong for a Christian to work in a distillery when he, himself, does not drink? Should a Christian rent a building to one who will sell liquor in it? Should he purchase stock in a distillery? What about dealing with a mutual company which invests in distillery stocks among others? Is it wrong for a farmer to sell corn to a distillery? Should he sell corn to a co-operative which sells part of its purchases to a distillery? "The problems are so complex you can't know what the will of God is," they say. Does this mean that we are simply to teach the gospel in general, then fold our hands and do nothing?

Admittedly, the problems are complex. However, the responsibility remains for Christians to make decisions, and they must act within various relationships. Therefore, the question must be asked, Who will have the better chance of finding the will of God, those who search for it diligently, or those who do not? Let it also be admitted that those who seek to find and follow the will of God will not always be able to be consistent. Society is complex, the ideal of the will of God is high, and we are still sinners. That is one reason we are grateful that salvation is by grace through faith. But even in falling far short of the best and in being inconsistent, those who study specific situations will come nearer finding and being able to follow the will of God than those who do not.

It must be recognized that in making a decision as to what the will of God is in a particular situation each individual, on the basis of his understanding of the Scriptures and under the leadership of the Holy Spirit, must be his own final authority. Here must come into focus the historic Baptist principle of individual freedom based on individual responsibility. Of course the individual would be quite foolish not to test his personal view against the thinking and insight of the larger Christian fellowship, but his decision does not have to conform to the decision of any group. No group will have the power to "tell" anyone what is the will of God for him, nor will it have any power to enforce conformity. Such pressure toward conformity leads to institutionalism in religion.

Recognizing that in any Christian fellowship and in any local church there will be many differences of opinion, the important thing is that the world will come to know that these Christians, even with their differing views, are expressing this view or are engaging in that action as *their witness to God!* They take their position not because of expediency, not because it is profitable, not because it will help them to be more successful, not even because it may help the church—but because they deeply believe this to be the will of God. This is their witness to their understanding of and commitment to the redeeming God.

The Christian who dares to seek and follow the will of God may frequently discover that he is wrong in his understanding of the will of God in a particular situation. In such cases he must be Christian enough to confess his error. Finite man is trying to understand the mind of the Infinite. Though saved, man is also a sinner and cannot have perfect knowledge. But this limitation need not leave him halting and fearful before decisions—fearful that he might make a wrong one. Again, the fact of justification by faith means that we are not saved by our ability to make right decisions. It also means that "God does not remove his presence or take away his love when a man makes a wrong decision. This fact sets a man free to decide bravely even at the risk of deciding wrongly." [4]

Therefore, the church should provide opportunities for these areas and relationships to be studied specifically and in depth. Under the leadership of the Holy Spirit, Christians might thus be led to those insights and convictions that would enable them to act more nearly according to the Christian ideal. Because people differ both in interest and in competency, some church members may want to study juvenile delinquency, others in the area of home relations, others in recreation, others in international relations, and so forth. Those of similar interest should get together to make a study in depth, using all available resources. Since all Christians will not be able to be in every study group, each group periodically would report to the total congregation the fruits of their study. This report would be discussed, openly and frankly, so that each individual would come to discover, under the leadership of the Holy Spirit, what he is to do and how he is to act in witnessing to God in any given area in his personal and social relations.

Certain situations might arise in the community or in society at large that might call for special attention. The church might then commission a group to make special study in this area and report to the church. It would be naive to suppose that in any given instance there would be unanimity of opinion. (To learn how to differ as Christians is one area where serious study needs to be made.) Yet each would be responsible for coming to his own conclusion as to what is the will of God and how he is to act to give his witness to God in this particular matter.

---

[4] Henderlite, *op. cit.*, p. 88.

The Christian in Society

In seeking to know and to follow the will of God, the Christian must not only be aware of his personal relations but also be keenly conscious of his social responsibilities. In religion our emphasis on the individual is proper, because each individual must give an account of himself to God and make his own response to God. However, we have generally failed to understand and emphasize adequately the corporate aspects of the gospel and of the life and work of the church.

There are some issues that cannot be settled by buttonholing people one by one and asking them to behave. Halford Luccock once said that if everyone in town dug a well in his back yard, the result would not be a municipal water system. A municipal water system can only be established by *corporate* action. Corporate evils usually can be eliminated only by corporate action.[5]

Southern Baptists reacted so violently against the "social gospel" movement of another generation that they have never given adequate attention to the social aspects of the gospel. The New Testament is filled with teachings concerning the social nature of the Christian life. Modern Christians must confess with shame that they have not been sufficiently aware of their social responsibilities. In the following statement Coe points out the type of social situation that must be the deep concern of every Christian.

In every bargain that I make, in every article that I use or consume, I traffic in human energies as well as in things, I relate myself to the health and happiness of men and women whom I have never seen. I take part in making their children what they become. To assume full responsibility for these acts of mine, to form a habit of seeing society as it is, and of tracing social causes and effects, and to think my very own moral life in community terms—these are the rudiments of an awakened, mature Christian conscience.[6]

The Christian must have a deep concern for the health con-

<hr>

[5] Rutenber, *op. cit.*, p. 108.
[6] George A. Coe, *A Social Theory of Religious Education* (New York: Charles Scribner's Sons, 1917), p. 105.

ditions in the community, for the educational standards, for the housing, and for wages paid to the working man. This concern may begin in one's own community, but it must reach out to people living in all the world. Those crowded together on the river boats in China, the people starving to death in Pakistan, those who lack educational opportunities in Indonesia, and the people living in the slums of one's own town—these are the Christian's responsibility.

As the Christian seeks to discover the will of God, he is often baffled by the complexity of problems in the world. The issues are never in terms of absolute good and absolute evil. For example, if Christians were to insist that other countries be given an opportunity to lift their standard of living by having a better chance to sell their products in this country, this might mean that we would have to change our own tariff laws. This could mean that thousands of Americans might be thrown out of work as goods from other countries would compete with American products. Thus, if we seek to help one group of people, we would hurt another group.

What is the will of God? The fact is that all of us at all times live our lives in ways that serve evil as well as good. This is merely an example of the magnitude of the moral dilemma that confronts Christians in the world. "Fritz Kreisler remarked not long ago that he never drinks a bottle of milk without realizing that he is taking it away from some child who needs it more than he does." [7] It is as Dean Willard Sperry said, "All of us— manufacturers, industrialists, bankers, brokers, hand workers, professors, doctors, ministers—are involved together in the moral muddle and the moral tragedy of our time." [8] However, because the problems are difficult is no reason for the Christian to despair. Rather, all the more must Christians come together to study these relationships specifically and in depth. For it is in the face of often conflicting "goods" that the individual

[7] Daniel Day Williams, God's Grace and Man's Hope (New York: Harper & Bros., 1949), p. 137.
[8] "Our Moral Chaos," Fortune, XXV, May, 1942, p. 108.

Christian must seek to find and express the will of God in his life.

Also as local congregations or as the people of God, Christians collectively have a serious social responsibility. Actually the church has a twofold function in the world. One function is that of conservation. It has the task to "hold fast that which is good." The church is not to have "itching ears" always seeking to "hear some new thing." Its task is to hear the word from God. It is not to follow foolish fads either in philosophic thought or in cultural change. But the second function is revolutionary in nature. The Christian gospel is the most revolutionary force in the world today, and the church is God's instrument for accomplishing his purpose. The tragedy is that having been called to this revolutionary task, the church is usually satisfied to focus on conservation.

While the church must be an instrument of God's judgment upon the evils of society, its voice must sound more than a negative note. "The relevance of Christianity to the whole social situation is overwhelmingly positive in character." It is "positive in the sense that it initiates a process." [9] In the recent racial turmoil in the South, for example, some churches that sponsored parochial schools (both Protestant and Roman Catholic) said, "We will desegregate our schools as soon as the cities in which they are located have done so." One outstanding Southern editor commented: "The question is, Can Christianity expect to be respected as a force for good if it is a follower in matters involving morality and law, rather than a leader? More and more the question is being posed from more and more pulpits: In moral and social issues, is it not the duty of Christianity to lead, not follow?" [10]

Thus, from a positive point of view Christians ought to be out in the forefront seeking changes in society that are in line

[9] D. R. Davies, *Secular Illusion or Christian Realism?* (New York: The Macmillan Co., 1949), p. 81.

[10] Ralph McGill, *The Atlanta Journal and The Atlanta Constitution*, XI, October 8, 1961, p. 1.

with righteousness and godliness. It has been stated that church members too often have identified the Christian life with simply living up to standards current in modern society—in morality, in business relations, in politics. Such a misconception could develop only because the church has not seriously sought to help the individual Christian to understand the implications of the Christian ethic for his personal life, his business relations, for labor-management relations, or for the myriad other daily relations.

This is not the way for the church to live in the world. If the purpose of the church is to do the will of God in the world, if the Christian ethic makes radical demands upon the lives of the followers of Christ, then one of the central assignments of the church is to find the practical implications of the Christian ethic in modern society and to take the lead in creating a social order that is increasingly in harmony with the will of God. This is not the "social gospel"; this is simply the gospel. These changes may come about primarily because Christians put them into practice in their own personal, business, and political relations. However, there will also be other avenues of action open to the Christian.

Too often the church has been simply a "moral club" composed of people who were willing to be "good." The church has not been "the body of Christ," determined to demonstrate in the world the same ideals Jesus demonstrated in "his body" in the days of his flesh. The radical element has been taken out of Christianity. This has made Christianity popular, but it has stripped it of its power. The only way for the church to recapture this power is for it to travel the hard and painful road back to the cross and demonstrate, as did Jesus, the radical demands of God—even at the expense of losing some members.

This does not mean at all that the church will be perfect or that it will be composed of those who are perfect. Those who compose the church are sinners saved by grace, but sinners nevertheless. Weaknesses, errors, and evil will be in the church and in the lives of individual Christians. Some will say we ought to clean up our own "house" before we seek to clean up society. As Christians we certainly need to exercise every care to seek to make our own "house" (church or personal life) as free from sin as is possible. We cannot wait, however, until the church is perfect before we seek to be Christian in society. Robert Spike says, "The realization that all men are sinners does not allow us the excuse of smiling indulgently and impartially upon bully and victim alike." [11] If this were to be our attitude, we could not send a missionary to the unsaved across the seas until all the homeland had been won.

"If the specific place of the laity in the world is at the frontiers where the real dialogue between Church and World becomes event, the laity at large needs a new orientation, a new grasp of the whole realm and scale of the reality of Christ, and a new equipment." [12] The word "dialogue" which Kraemer uses is, indeed, a happy choice. Dialogue means mutual exchange. It pictures Christians approaching the problems of the world, of society, and of the spirit in deep humility. Since we cannot claim to know "the" answers to all difficult problems, in dialogue we will both speak and listen; we will seek to teach; we will also learn. We will not undertake sweeping social reforms. We will try to make sure that both we and the world ask the right questions. Most church members, even the most faithful ones, do not now have this "new orientation" and this "new equipment" to enable them to have a serious dialogue and encounter with the world. To equip the layman for this task is one of the supreme tasks of the church.

To help Christians secure this orientation and equipment, the major areas of human relationships should be made a major part of the curriculum for young people and adults. Our denomination, along with other religious and secular groups, should seek to identify those trends that are now or may become crucial issues in human relations within the next ten to

---

[11] Robert W. Spike, *In but Not of the World* (New York: Association Press, 1957), p. 105.

[12] Kraemer, *op. cit.*, p. 172.

twenty years. These issues should then be included in the curriculum to be studied and discussed *in light of the gospel* before they come to have personal and emotional involvements. The race issue could have been discussed with little difficulty fifteen years ago. By not making a serious depth study of this problem at that time in the light of the gospel, the church sinned away its day of grace. This must not happen again. The attitude of the average church member is too often only a reflection of those values and standards current in society. No wonder the life of the Christian has not been different from the life of the unregenerate "good people" in the world!

Should the Church Deal with Controversial Issues?

Many Christians believe sincerely that certain areas of social and human relations are not within the task of the church. To them it is the task of the church to preach the gospel. To deal with explosive and divisive problems would do far more harm than good. Therefore, we have a responsibility to face the question: Should the church deal with controversial questions?

In the throes of reality, to ask this question is the same as asking: Should the church deal with the crucial issues of life? People are not bothered by easy, simple, black-and-white questions. It is precisely because problems are complex and controversial that they become the crucial issues of life. It is within these issues that man lives and moves and has his being. He does not escape these questions simply because they are difficult. He has to answer them, and he does answer them, one way or another—either with the benefit of the Christian perspective or without it.

To deal directly and in depth with these controversial and difficult issues is one of the fundamental tasks of the church. If the church is truly a *koinonia,* if there is genuine concern to know the will of God, then it is within this type of fellowship where these difficult questions can best be discussed. If they cannot be faced within this fellowship of love and concern, where can they be discussed? Not to be able to consider difficult, even explosive, issues within the church is tacit admission that Christ is not *the answer*.

The church cannot afford to ignore these problems. The world has to face these issues and deal with them in some manner—around the conference tables, in labor union meetings, in legislative halls, and in ward offices of mercenary politicians. Decisions will be made. Action will be taken. Does Christ, through his church, have no word to speak? Is there no light from above to shine in our darkness to give guidance? If the church is going to perform her real ministry *in the world*, then she must get into the arena, of life and "get her hands dirty" grappling with real issues.

The church must learn not to be afraid of honest differences of opinion. According to our study of the history of religious movements, when they were vital and dynamic, differences of opinion were honestly held and freely expressed. But institutionalism had set in when positions became crystallized and thought and expression were stifled. External harmony was achieved, but experiential religion was lost.

True Christian fellowship does not mean that everyone must think alike. It does demand genuine acceptance and respect on the part of all involved, even in the midst of differences of opinion. Seemingly we have not as yet developed this kind of *koinonia* in our churches. In a recent study of adults in Southern Baptist churches it was found that 78 per cent of the Sunday school members said they did not feel free to express an opinion which differed from that of their teacher.[13]

As long as people live in a real world they will have to deal with controversial questions. They cannot be avoided for they are an integral and inevitable part of life. Therefore, Christians seeking to know the will of God have a right to expect the church to provide some guidance in these areas.

---

[13] Ernest J. Loessner, "The Expressed Religious Education Needs of Adults of Two Contrasting Educational Levels, with the Teachers' Perceptions of Their Expressions of Needs." Unpublished doctoral thesis, Indiana University, Bloomington, Indiana, pp. 72-75.

Is not this the vehicle God has chosen above all others to "make his way known among men, his saving health among all nations"? But the expectation fades to hope, and hope gives way to futility as the bitter truth becomes evident in a thousand ways: the church is not a community of people through whom God speaks so much as it is an institution which echoes the very society which is toppling. One sees next to no evidence that the church is willing to be laid upon the altar as a sacrifice in order to manifest God's reconciling work.[14]

Because of this the church is failing to be an effective instrument through which God is able to speak his word in the world and to the world. The church is simply being ignored by the world. Dr. H. H. Hobbs wrote pertinently on this problem.

Recently David Lawrence, a syndicated columnist, wrote an article dealing with the intensive and extensive efforts on the part of the "Reds" to infiltrate every vital area of American and international life. . . . He says that it is not accidental that Communism concentrates in three fields, "education, unions, entertainment," and then the shocker. "These are the areas where ideas flourish and thinking patterns are formed." When I read that statement, I became really worried, not about Communism so much as about Christianity. He did not include churches in "the areas where ideas flourish and thinking patterns are formed." . . . Can it be that they do not regard our churches as worthy opponents? . . . Are our churches so impotent as to be ignored? Is their influence upon the vital issues of life so small as to render them free from Communist consideration? Is our message held in contempt by them as not coming to grips with the fundamental needs of men caught in the machinery of the social order? . . . My concern is not that Communists shall invade us, but that they shall ignore us as unworthy of consideration. The Christian who is having an easy lot is not necessarily the best Christian. Never was Jesus more pleasing to God as His beloved Son than when He was hanging on a cross amid the curses and opposition of the enemies of God.[15]

If the church is going to come to "grips with the fundamental needs of men caught in the machinery of the social order," if the church is going to contribute in any meaningful manner

---

[14] Meister, *op. cit.*, p. 256.
[15] "I'm Really Worried," *Western Recorder*, August 18, 1960, p. 3.

to those areas where "ideas flourish and thinking patterns are formed," then it must deal with controversial isues.

To fail to deal with controversial questions may reveal a desire to be safe in order to be popular—another indication of creeping institutionalism. The church that will not face these issues constructively cannot be an adequate channel for God's word and work. Recently a Southern Baptist editor wrote to this point, "Southern Baptists . . . claim to have God's answer for today's world, but actually [we] are sleeping through a world revolution by remaining silent on integration, labor, and other burning social issues because they are controversial or because they might hurt the Cooperative Program." [16]

Some church and denominational leaders are genuinely concerned about communicating the gospel in its full meaning, but often there appears to be a *greater* concern to avoid anything that might disrupt the fellowship. This attitude shows up in the statement, "We don't want to break the 'cord' that binds us to the people." Such an attitude is understandable. Can we help people if we "break" with them? Yet, as reasonable as it is, this attitude, if carried to an extreme, can lead to institutionalism. This attitude may see the task of the church as only to "preach the gospel" in the abstract, or in general, or in terms of individual salvation without ever coming to grips with some of the larger issues of life.

It is reasonable for one to say, "The church should 'lean over backward' to keep the peace." Our difficulty today, however, is that through the years the church has "leaned over backward" so much to keep the peace until finally she is lying flat on her back. The church lives at peace in a sinful society because she is not doing enough to give entrenched evils of society any real trouble. These entrenched evils simply ignore the church. The church is able to carry on her work in peace, but peace has been bought at too high a price.

This matter is directly related also to the problem of a regenerate church membership. That is, when a church begins

<hr>

[16] C. R. Daley, "Daley Observations," *Western Recorder*, May 25, 1961, p. 4

to "let down the bars" to receive members whose lives in reality are dominated by secular considerations rather than by the will of God, the church will find more and more that it can preach less and less of the Christian gospel without disrupting the fellowship. The gospel can be proclaimed in its fulness and power only within the framework of a regenerate church membership.

Therefore, in order to have a vital and experiential religion, the prevailing attitude must be reversed. That is, we ought to have a genuine concern to maintain the fellowship, but the *greater concern ought to be that we will be faithful in communicating the gospel in its fulness.* There seems to be an almost compulsive attitude and reasoned conclusion on the part of leadership and membership alike that the church must do nothing that would cause it to become unpopular. To do so might cause us to "lose all we had gained," we hear it said. But a serious question must be faced honestly: Have all our gains really been gains? Or is it possible that in the midst of all our gains we may unconsciously be losing something that is far more fundamental to the New Testament faith than all our external advancement?

It must be understood that the question here is one of emphasis; both aspects of the dilemma are worthy and must be taken into account. However, in the New Testament it seems that the primary emphasis was placed on the faithful communication and application of the gospel rather than upon what people's response to it might be. It was the gospel to which people, both in and out of the church, had to respond either for healing or for judgment. In the midst of our situation, there is an uneasy feeling developing in the minds of some that

the church is more eager to save itself and its . . . institutions in this culture than it is to give away the redemptive secret. Their intuition also tells them a truth which the church tries to hide, even from itself: that to give away the redemptive secret would mean nailing the church with its institutions to the Cross.[17]

---

[17] Meister, *op. cit.*, p. 256.

The Cross—A Present Reality

Perhaps, then, the fundamental question Christians need to answer is whether they are willing to "take up their cross" with Jesus in order to accomplish the will of God in the world. Through the centuries the cross has been central in the Christian faith. On it Jesus died that we might live. By the cross he did for man what man could never do for himself. It is no wonder that "the emblem of suffering and shame" is central in the love and devotion of Christians. But the cross is more than an event of the past; it is a present reality which the Christian must experience. "I am crucified with Christ: nevertheless I live; yet not I, but Christ liveth in me" (Gal. 2:20). Nor is it only a "one-time" experience; it is a way of life. As Paul said, "I die daily" (1 Cor. 15:31).

For many people any tragedy, disaster, or affliction is considered a "cross" which one must bear. But this interpretation mistakes a "cross" for what Paul called a "thorn in the flesh." A "thorn in the flesh" is some affliction or tragedy which is *unavoidable*. The individual had no control over the situation, no choice in the matter. The cross, on the other hand, is always *avoidable*. The individual can refuse to accept the cross; he can refuse to suffer; he can refuse to die. Thus, to "take up one's cross" means *voluntarily* to accept and follow a course of action that will lead to suffering and perhaps death in order to do the will of God.

Now, how does the cross contribute to an understanding of the nature and meaning of the Christian life?

The cross means sharing the suffering of Christ to the last and to the fullest. Only a man thus totally committed in discipleship can experience the meaning of the cross. The cross is there, right from the beginning, he has only got to pick it up; there is no need for him to go out and look for a cross for himself, no need for him deliberately to run after suffering. . . . When Christ calls a man, he bids him come and die.[18]

---

[18] Dietrich Bonhoeffer, *The Cost of Discipleship* (2nd ed.; New York: The Macmillan Co., 1959), pp. 78-79.

The cross, then, says that suffering is a real and inevitable part of the Christian life. The Christian does not have to seek suffering. It will come to him as he seeks to be positively Christian, as he seeks to express a Christian witness in the world rather than to remain silent in the midst of the controversial issues of life.

The possibility of suffering as a necessary aspect of the Christian life is not suggested lightly. It should be contemplated with utmost seriousness. It will call for a drastic change in the attitude of most church members. They recall that Christians of other centuries were called on to suffer, but they do not realize that being truly Christian in today's world may lead to suffering for Christ's sake. Since the Christian life involves making oneself available as an instrument of the will of God both in judgment upon the evils and injustices of a sinful society and in redemptive love for the oppressed, Christians will be brought inevitably into sharp conflict with the world. It may be that the church cannot be the true church unless it is in conflict with the world.

The early Christians did not recoil from but rather sought to create the occasions of faith conflict, for such occasions gave them opportunity to declare their faith in the Gospel of Jesus Christ. The great Christian preachers and theologians engaged the spokesman of the pagan religions and philosophies while the ordinary everyday Christian laymen assumed their missionary responsibilities in the market place. At the risk of persecution they moved among the masses contesting every expressed or implied pagan loyalty while inviting all and sundry to embrace the "illicit subversive" Christian faith.[19]

While Christians must always contend for the faith in the spirit of Christ and for the purpose of redemption, the conflict may arouse emotions and stiff opposition. When the livelihood of human exploiters is seriously threatened, they will unleash all their forces against their critics. Whenever the will of God comes in conflict with the way of the world, a cross is always raised; and the Christian must decide whether to "take

---

[19] Perry, *op. cit.*, p. 2.

up his cross" or to reject it. The race issue raised a cross in our society. Christians faced it and, by and large, refused to "take it up"; the suffering involved was too great. Jesus made it clear

beyond all doubt that the "must" of suffering applies to his disciples no less than to himself. Just as Christ is Christ only in virtue of his suffering and rejection, so the disciple is a disciple only in so far as he shares his Lord's suffering and rejection and crucifixion. Discipleship means adherence to the person of Jesus, and therefore submission to the law of Christ which is the law of the cross.[20]

In today's preaching suffering is usually only a point in a sermon and not a living reality. But if suffering which comes from conflict with evils of the world is a necessary part of the Christian life today, then pastors and denominational leaders will need to brace themselves against the loss of some members. Inevitably, some will "walk no more" with us. Was this not exactly what the multitude did to Jesus? "Strait is the gate, and narrow is the way," he said, "which leadeth unto life, and few there be that find it" (Matt. 7:14). Conflict with the world might mean also serious losses in financial support for the church. It may be that because of the very severity of its demands, Christianity can never become a mass movement.

Facing such a possibility, church leaders may well ask: "Is taking a positive stand on some particular issue worth taking the chance of alienating some of our people and possibly disrupting our total program?" The answer the modern churches have given, in the main, is "no." Most have chosen to "play it safe" and to follow the path of "peace at any price." The price the church has paid has been to evade the cross— the same temptation Jesus faced—to accomplish the will of God without suffering. But Jesus taught that an individual (or church) lives only by dying. This means getting on the cross, not evading it.

We want to be Christian without a cross. We want to be

---

[20] Bonhoeffer, *op. cit.*, p. 77.

safe without suffering. We rationalize, compromise, water-down, and become like those about us. Not so with Peter and John. Coming into conflict with their world, they said, "We cannot but speak the things which we have seen and heard" (Acts 4:20). They had good reason to follow the principle of expediency. They could have reasoned that considerable prog-ress had been made through the early preaching of the gospel. Perhaps they should slow down and consolidate their gains. They might be able to win even more of the Jews if they did not get into serious conflict with the authorities. Why risk antagonizing them? After all, one could not do much preaching in prison. But expediency was not a guiding principle in early Christianity. Instead they preached; they gave a radical ex-pression of the Christian life. To be sure they suffered; many of them died. But they changed their world.

Today, we do not suffer; we do not die; but neither do we change our world. Why? Because we who claim to be Christian face the cross and back away from it. The only way the church can live in peace in a sinful society is for it to refuse to be the church. This is exactly what the modern church is doing. It is seeking to save itself as an institution (certainly a worthy desire) but it is losing its life. Even with the church, "who-soever shall seek to save his life shall lose it" (Luke 17:33). The church, too, must die to self if it would live.

This condition calls for serious discussion among all who are searching for experiential religion. We don't want to lose numbers simply for the sake of losing numbers. There is no inherent value in small numbers just as there is no inherent evil in large numbers. We must be careful also to avoid de-veloping a martyr complex. A course of action must not be fol-lowed that will lead to suffering, simply suffering for its own sake. On the other hand, we must make sure that our desire to avoid a martyr complex is not merely a cover-up for cow-ardice. We must make sure that our desire not to hurt anyone or to lose any members is not a rationalization on our part to avoid doing battle in the world and with the world.

So the church is faced with a crucial and difficult question. This is one of those complex questions where an answer has to be made and will be made in some manner. Shall we continue our church program and our Christian life pretty much along our present line with perhaps some minor modifications? Or is there a more radical change necessary in order to come closer to the New Testament pattern?

Part III
How One Enters the Christian Life

8

The Nature of Man and
the Task of the Church

Perhaps the outstanding exponent of "liberal" theology in the first part of the twentieth century to deal seriously with the problems of the nature of man and of sin was Frederick R. Tennant.[1] Most theologians and religious educators of that period were influenced by him either directly or indirectly. The religious educators also were influenced by John Dewey. These "optimists" rejected the doctrine of original sin and held to a belief in the essential goodness of human nature. They minimized or denied the reality of sin in the nature of man. In fact, the "progressive" religious educators generally avoided using the term "sin" in their study of man. Along with this rosy view of human nature they held that a child was in the kingdom of God. George A. Coe, one of the leading exponents of progressive religious education said in his book, *A Social Theory of Religious Education,* "To Tertullian's argument that the soul is naturally Christian we may now add that the child is naturally Christian."[2] In another book, he said: "Normal child development, then, takes place entirely within the kingdom of grace."[3]

The question for the religious educator was not, "Will this child ever be converted to God?" but, "Will he ever be converted away from God?" They developed a philosophy of edu-

---

[1] Among his writings are: *The Sources of the Doctrines of the Fall and Original Sin, The Origin and Propagation of Sin,* and *Philosophical Theology* (2 vols.).

[2] *Op. cit.,* p. 145.

[3] George A. Coe, *Education in Religion and Morals* (New York: Fleming H. Revell Co., 1904), p. 47.

cation based on this theology and engaged in a vigorous program of moralistic character education. Their mistake was that they supposed ignorance to be the chief enemy of man when, in reality, man's fundamental problem is that there is disorder at the very center of his nature. Man might overcome his ignorance, but he is powerless to change the disorder of his nature. Thus, both the program and the philosophy were inadequate because they were based upon an erroneous theology.

The Human Predicament

This romantic view of man with its promise of evolving progress was broken against the realities of war and depression. Whereas formerly the effort had been made to understand man wholly in terms of psychology and philosophy, there now came to be an effort to understand man in biblical terms. The reality of sin as an element in human experience was recognized as fact.

The biblical doctrine of man differs from all other views of man in two significant respects, namely, in the heights to which it raises man as a creature made in the "image of God," and in the depths to which it plunges man as a result of sin. The human predicament cannot be understood apart from the fact of sin. This is man's tragedy! "All man's troubles stem from this one source. None can be solved ultimately unless the relationship to God, broken through sin, is restored." [4]

The essence of sin in man is viewed differently by different writers. Some see the essence of sin as pride. Others see it as anxiety, injustice, or sensuality. Still others refer to it as self-contradiction. Yet all agree that sin, in its expression, is rebellion—rebellion against God. God created man "a little lower than the angels" (or God) with freedom. Man refused to admit or accept his creatureliness. Man chose to defy God and sought to make himself God in his own life. Sin is "the revolt

---

[4] George W. Forell, *The Protestant Faith* (Englewood Cliffs, N. J., Prentice-Hall, Inc., 1960), pp. 142-143.

of the creature against the Creator; thus it is not something negative, it is a positive negation. Sin is defiance, arrogance, the desire to be equal with God, emancipation, a deliberate severance from the hand of God. This is the explanation of the nature of sin and its origin." [5]

One of the major problems with which theologians have struggled in seeking to understand the nature of man has been that of original sin. Is sin inherently part and parcel of the nature of man? As would be expected, many and varied views have been given in answer to this question.[6] Reinhold Niebuhr was the American theologian who contributed most to the revival of concern in the fall of man and the doctrine of original sin. According to Niebuhr "the utopian illusions and sentimental aberrations of modern liberal culture are really all derived from the basic error of negating the fact of original sin." [7] However, he reacted quite vigorously against the idea that original sin means "inherited corruption." This, he said, would violate the freedom of man and would thus cause man not to be responsible for his sin. He made the distinction that sin is "inevitable" but not "necessary." In this way he sought to keep in balance the fact of sin, the universality of sin, and man's responsibility for sin.

Bishop Newbigin, on the other hand, seems to imply that original sin is transmitted in the biological procreation of the race. He says that the newborn babe does not begin life with a nature that is finely balanced in its predisposition to good and evil. Rather his nature is heavily weighted toward evil. "Every human being thus inherits a nature which is already tainted by sin, and every man also commits sin for which he is individually responsible." [8] Walter Horton would agree:

---

[5] Emil Brunner, *Man in Revolt*, trans. Olive Wyon (Philadelphia: The Westminster Press, 1947), p. 129.

[6] Cf. H. Shelton Smith, *Changing Conceptions of Original Sin* (New York: Charles Scribner's Sons, 1955), for a survey of American theological thought since 1750.

[7] Niebuhr, *op. cit.*, p. 273, n. 4.

[8] Lesslie Newbigin, *Sin and Salvation* (London: S.C.M. Press, Ltd., 1956), p. 38.

I believe that orthodox Christianity represents a profound insight into the whole human predicament. I believe that the basic human difficulty *is* that perversion of the will, that betrayal of divine trust, which is called sin; and I believe that sin *is* in a sense a racial disease, transmissible from generation to generation.[9]

Three major points should be noted in the concept of original sin: First, there is the totality of sin, that is, it is the whole of man that is infected by sin, not just a part of him. This does not mean total depravity in the sense that man is thereby incapable of doing any good thing. It means that man's every thought and act is contaminated by the fact of sin. Second, there is the solidarity of sin. It is not just a question of the sinfulness of the individual; sin is characteristic of the whole human race. "It is the disposition of every infant, every adult, every social group (including the organized churches and sects), and every culture to affirm its own wants and will as ultimate." [10] Third, there is the " 'inevitability' of sin—every man is by 'fallen' nature a sinner." [11]

Although original sin is a fact in the nature and experience of man, man is still responsible for his own sin. "Sin is a personal and responsible act. It is a personal revolt against God, which is aggravated by society and its shortcomings but which is nevertheless our personal responsibility. In fact, the shortcomings of society are in turn the result of personal failures. And so we are involved in a vicious circle." [12] Reinhold Niebuhr, in his analysis of the nature of original sin, was particularly careful to insist that the freedom of man is in no way impaired, and thus man remains a responsible creature. "The Christian estimate of human evil is so serious precisely because it places evil at the very centre of human personality: in the will." [13] Likewise, Brunner points out that sin is not merely

---

[9] *Realistic Theology* (New York: Harper & Bros., 1934), p. 56.

[10] T. E. Jessop *et al.*, *The Christian Understanding of Man* (London: George Allen & Unwin, Ltd., 1938), p. 77.

[11] Frederic Greeves, *The Meaning of Sin* (London: The Epworth Press, 1956), p. 31.

[12] Forell, *op. cit.*, pp. 138-139.

[13] *Op. cit.*, p. 16.

something which is lacking in man but is a "positive negation" for which he is responsible. "All non-Biblical doctrine makes evil harmless and excuses man, whereas the Bible shows up sin in all its terrible character and makes man 'inexcusable.' No Fate, no metaphysical constitution, no weakness of his nature, but himself, man, in the centre of his personality, is made responsible for his sin." [14] Man is a sinner! This is the verdict of the theologians. No philosophy of religious education and no program of the church can be adequate that does not place this fundamental fact at its center.

Man's Need Met

God takes sin with utmost seriousness. He refuses to be the God that the masses have tried to make him be: an indulgent grandfather who closes his eyes to the sins of the children. Sin is not some slight wrongdoing that deserves a "slap on the wrist." Sin is rebellion at the center of the nature of man. Thus the plight of man in sin, from God's perspective, is desperate.

Because of sin man is enslaved in a depravity from which only God can free him. A radical remedy is needed. The tragedy of man is that, sinner as he is, within himself he is powerless to solve his fundamental problem. He may struggle vigorously but he struggles in vain to lift himself by his own bootstraps. It is only within this framework that the *good news* of the gospel can be truly understood and appreciated. *God has acted supremely in behalf of sinful man!* As George Buttrick has said, "the most wonderful thing has happened!"

To help man in his desperate need, God always takes the initiative. God is a seeking God. In the fifteenth chapter of Luke Jesus says that God is like a shepherd who seeks after the one lost sheep; he is like the woman who searches for a lost coin; he is like a father who yearns after his lost son. To seek after lost man is not simply God's purpose; it is his very nature.

Just as the biblical view of man is unique at two points, so

[14] *Op. cit.*, p. 131.

the biblical view of man's atonement is unique at two points. First, there is the emphasis on a seeking God offering salvation as a free gift. This "pearl of great price," which a man should be willing to sell all to obtain, is offered to man as a gift. Indeed it cannot be purchased. There is nothing man can do to earn or merit it. He must receive it as a free gift. Baillie made it clear that the New Testament emphasis on free forgiveness to penitent sinners goes much farther than anything that had been taught by prophet or rabbi. "Here is the 'reconciliation' which wipes out our trespasses, but we contribute nothing to the process: 'It is all of God'." [15]

In the second place, there is the emphasis on the costliness of this salvation. The sin-offering was the "Lamb of God" and this Lamb was God's own Son. "He . . . spared not his own Son, but delivered him up for us all" (Rom. 8:32). "For God so loved the world, that he gave his only begotten Son" (John 3:16). God is inexorable love. If one has betrayed this love, it is the ultimate betrayal. "That is what has to be wiped out, and such an 'atonement' must be the most difficult, the most supernatural, the costliest thing in the world." [16] The cross stands forever as an evidence of the seriousness with which God views sin. It also stands as an evidence of the desperate plight of man "out of Christ." If sin is merely some minor malady, if man in his natural state is not doomed and without hope, if the destiny of man "out of Christ" is not something which is utterly abhorrent to the nature of God and completely tragic for man himself, then God's anguish on the cross was not necessary nor does the cross have any particular meaning. "To create the heavens and the earth costs Him no labour, no anguish; to take away the sin of the world costs Him His own life-blood." [17]

God has acted but man must react. God offers a free gift, but man must receive it. Because sin is personal, confession and

---

[15] D. M. Baillie, *God Was in Christ* (New York: Charles Scribner's Sons, 1948), p. 178.
[16] *Ibid.*, p. 174.
[17] Newbigin, *op. cit.*, p. 32.

acceptance must also be personal. Not even God can remove the guilt of man apart from man's personal response. Even in this sacred experience God must honor man's freedom; otherwise he would be less than the man he was before the "fall." Newbigin points out that when the psalmist cried, "Wash me thoroughly from mine iniquity, and cleanse me from my sin," this was possible only because he also said, "I acknowledge my transgressions: and my sin is ever before me" (Psalm 51:2-3). "Sin can never be removed until the sinner acknowledges it, confesses it, and repudiates it." [18] A choice must be made. "I have set before thee this day life . . . and death . . . therefore choose life" (Deut. 30:15-19). Man's decision determines his destiny.

In this relationship of man and God there is a point beyond which the educational processes cannot go. It is possible for us to bring people to the Christian fellowship, and through Bible study and the proclamation of the Word, we may lead them "to the edge of the abyss, but only by God's grace do they make the leap of faith." [19] Or as Iris Cully puts it, "there is a definite aloneness to this encounter, even though it may take place within a group and be prepared for by the surrounding fellowship of the church." [20] In the aloneness of this encounter it is God who works his work of transforming grace. The processes of education may lead up to this encounter but they cannot produce it.

One does not come into the Christian life by chance or automatically as the result of teaching or nurture. One comes into the Christian life in response to the call of God through a conscious choice and surrender of his life. Although it need not be a cataclysmic or highly emotional experience, this venture must be a conscious and definite response of the individual to the call of God. Its beginnings may be so small and come so early in life that the individual cannot recall the first aware-

[18] *Ibid.*, p. 34.
[19] Miller, *op. cit.*, p. 193.
[20] *The Dynamics of Christian Education* (Philadelphia: The Westminster Press, 1958), p. 144.

ness. But in the salvation relationship the individual must come to have a mature understanding of the nature of the Christian life in terms of the mission and ministry to which God is calling, and there must be a mature and conscious acceptance of the lordship of Christ in which the individual surrenders himself to be an instrument to carry out God's mission and ministry in the world. Becoming a Christian is not something shallow or superficial.

This type of relationship with God is the only sufficient foundation for experiential religion. The church cannot change the world unless it is composed of changed people. This change must be a radical transformation and not a shallow reformation. It cannot occur on the basis of mere nurture but must result from an encounter with the living God.

Incarnate Witness

If man is sinner, if he stands under the "wrath of God," if he is "without hope," if God has acted to provide a way of redemption by making the supreme sacrifice in the gift of his Son, then the fundamental task of the church is to bring sinful man into right relationship with the redeeming God. The doctrine of election indicates that this is the reason God is calling to himself a "peculiar people." It is to this mission God's people must respond.

The primary task of the church is to witness. An important part of this witness will be given in and through the church. But the doctrine of the priesthood of all believers indicates that the major witness is to be given by Christians *in the world.* A major weakness of the modern church is that it has depended almost exclusively upon holding services in the church building as the means of winning a world to Christ. These services have consisted primarily of verbal witnessing, either teaching or preaching. But the masses of the people were not at the church! The service had no impact upon them! Without minimizing the importance of teaching or preaching, it must be said that unless the gospel becomes incarnate in the lives of church members, "the world" will never see or hear. It is quite probable that this incarnate witness must be given to the world before the world will ever listen to or be able to understand a verbal witness.

Culbert G. Rutenber gives a helpful analysis at this point. He says a witness may be one of three types. He may be an observer, as one who observes an automobile accident and testifies to what he saw. Or he may have been a passenger in the car who was not hurt himself but can tell how badly his fellow passengers were hurt. Or he may be one of those who was seriously injured and who bears in his body vivid evidence of the accident. "A Christian witness is one who is himself part of the evidence of that to which he testifies." [21] He then illustrates this point by the experience of the early Christians in the book of Acts. At first the Christians were commanded to wait for the coming of the Holy Spirit. With the coming of the Holy Spirit a marvelous thing happened to them. They went out and all the people heard the gospel in their own language. The people were amazed and they began to ask questions, "What does this mean?" (Acts 2:12). After Peter preached, many believed. In chapter 3, Peter and John were accosted by a beggar. Again they demonstrated the power of Christ, and again the people were astonished at what they *saw*, and again Peter had an opportunity to interpret verbally the meaning of what they *saw*. In chapter 4 the apostles witness brought persecution, but even this served as an opportunity for further witness.

What is God trying to tell us in all this? The answer marks the end of some of our most cherished and damaging prejudices and the beginning—God grant—of a new understanding of the biblical meaning of witness. Witness cannot be carried by words alone. If it is the love of Christ to which we would witness, we must *become* the love of Christ in incarnation and effectual deed in order to speak meaningfully of it.[22]

---

[21] *Op. cit.*, p. 116.
[22] *Ibid.*, p. 118.

Thus social action is not *mere* social action; it is a way of *witnessing* in the world! It is one form of evangelism and it may be the most powerful form of evangelism. Christian social action is a prime means of the Christian to demonstrate the transforming power of God.

Why did Jesus link love of neighbor with love for God? Was it simply because this is a high ethical code a Christian ought to live by? No! Its purpose is redemptive! When a Christian genuinely loves his neighbor as himself, when he desires the good and welfare for his neighbor that he desires for himself—and expresses this in action—eventually his neighbor is going to ask, "Why? Why do you do this for me? Why do you live this way?" Having thus given his witness to God by his actions, he then has the chance of giving his witness to God verbally. His verbal witness can be most effective only after he has given his witness by his actions. Thus, whether he is a business executive, a factory worker, an insurance salesman, or a farmer, the totality of a Christian's life must be his witness to God.

It is possible that while the Christian is giving this witness, the "neighbor" may take unfair advantage of him. In an evil social order where "sin abounds," while the Christian is seeking to "love his neighbor as himself" and thus give his witness to God, the "neighbor" may beat him in a business deal. The Christian may lose money. To put it differently, the "neighbor" may "nail him to a cross." This is a chance the Christian must take. But even on a cross the Christian still gives his witness to God. In times past, God has used a cross to break the heart of sinners, and perchance—not always, but perchance—the neighbor will come back at some time and ask, "Why? Why do you live this way? What is it you have?" And then the Christian will have an opportunity to witness verbally to the redemptive love of God. But whether the neighbor comes back or not, this is still the way the Christian must live. Indeed, this is not only the *way* the Christian must live, it is his *reason* for living!

This kind of living is not the "social gospel." Man is able to find the solution to the problems that are involved in his horizontal relationships only when he finds a transforming relationship with the eternal God. But the Christian has a witness to give, a mission to fulfil, a ministry to perform that must be carried out in the social order of which he is a part.

Some churches and groups are seriously attempting to give such a witness in the world and are being successful in their efforts. Elton Trueblood in *The Company of the Committed* calls attention to a number of these who are giving creative and daring expression to their Christian faith in the world. He suggests that the church needs to train "penetration groups" whose task would be to penetrate the world in such areas as the colleges and universities, politics, journalism, capital, labor, and indeed every major area of life.

It need hardly be said that all of these new contemporary tasks are so arduous that they will never appeal to those who want easy lives or who desire to follow only in well-tried and conventional Christian channels. Many of the experiments in these new fields will fail, as scientific experiments frequently do, but that is how progress is possible. In any case, herein lies the relevant ministry for our time.[23]

Verbal Witness

The Christian's testimony must be incarnate but it must also be a testimony given by word. "The spoken word is never really effective unless it is backed up by a life, but it is also true that the living deed is never adequate without the support which the spoken word can provide." [24] Thus, one of the central tasks of the Christian is to give a witness in word.

In at least four areas today's courtroom witness and the Christian witness are similar. *First,* in a court of law the task of the witness is simply to relate the pertinent facts as he saw or experienced them. He is not expected to convince the jury or argue the case. All that is required, expected, or permitted

[23] New York: Harper & Bros., 1961, p. 88.
[24] *Ibid.,* p. 53.

of the witness is to testify to the facts. Likewise, the responsibility of the Christian witness is simply to bear testimony to the facts as he has experienced them. It is not his responsibility to convince the person that the Christian way is right. Of course it is the deepest desire of the Christian that the person will become convicted and convinced, but in the salvation experience there is a point beyond which the Christian cannot go. He can only bear witness to what he knows and what he has experienced.

For this reason it would be well if we would replace the term "soul-winner" with the term "witness." Strictly speaking "soul-winning" is the work of God, not man. Whether the individual to whom we witness comes into a saving relationship depends upon the encounter he has with Christ under the convicting power of the Holy Spirit. The danger is that a person who views himself as a "soul-winner" sometimes invades the sacred arena where God and man face each other for possible encounter and surrender. In his zeal to "win a soul to Christ" through subtle pressures he induces the individual to "make a profession" which may be only verbal and superficial. The Christian's witness will be as fervent and intelligent as he can make it. But the response the individual makes is his own responsibility.

On the other hand, some warn that if a Christian feels no responsibility for the outcome of his witness, he may become indifferent to the outcome. But a person cannot be a Christian witness and not be concerned about its fruit. Jesus was concerned about the outcome of his witness to the rich young ruler, but he in no way violated his freedom.

In the *second* place, the legal witness is expected to testify only to those facts or events which he has seen or heard. He is not expected to know all the facts in the case. Not having seen all the events connected with the case does not invalidate either his reliability or value as a witness. He is a witness, not because he knows everything, but because he does know something.

This is true also of the Christian witness. It is not expected that he should know everything about the Christian faith before he gives his witness. When called to witness, many Christians object: "I'm afraid I wouldn't know what to say," or "I'm afraid they would ask me a question about the Bible I could not answer." But the Christian witness is not expected to know all there is to be known about the Bible. He is not expected to be a specialist in theology. He is not expected to be able to answer all the person's questions. He is not expected to be able to refute all the person's objections. There are many things about the "case for Christianity" which the Christian does not know and about which he cannot testify. As a witness he simply testifies as to what he knows, as to what he experienced, as to what happened to *him*. This is all that is expected; this is all that is required.

Third, the legal witness has a responsibility to testify; he has no other choice. If he has pertinent information on the case, he is expected to give his witness to the facts as he knows them. So important is this in our legal system that a witness can be required to testify, or else suffer punishment. The Christian, too, has a responsibility to witness. There are no legal requirements; none should be needed. What he has to tell is good news! It is the kind of witness every man should be thrilled to give.

Fourth, the legal witness must have some firsthand knowledge of, or contact with, the case under consideration. There may be a hundred thousand people in the city, but only those who saw the automobile accident or had pertinent information about it are called to be witnesses. Likewise, a person cannot be a witness to Christ unless he has had a firsthand experience with Christ. As a witness he is expected to testify as to what happened to him. If nothing has happened to him then he has nothing about which he can give a witness. In light of the large number of church members who never make any effort to give any type of verbal witness, some serious and disturbing questions can be raised at this point.

Outreach for the Unreached

To give both the incarnate and the verbal witness, the church must be involved in a vigorous and persistent program of outreach for those who are unreached. At this point those who have kept this emphasis on outreach central in their ministry deserve a genuine word of commendation. This does not mean that all has been done that should have been done or could have been done. It does mean that outreach for those who are unreached has been a matter of deep concern, and a serious effort has been made to match the need with action. Yet an overwhelming task still remains.

It is the world that needs Christ. It was the world for which Christ died (Luke 5:32). The sin of the Jews—the sin for which they were rejected—is being repeated in the life of many modern churches. If Christians fail to reach out, to seek those who are unreached, if they minister only to their own, they are failing to fulfil the essential purpose of their election.

Yet, this is precisely what is happening. Leaders of almost all denominations are beginning to express alarm over this failure of the church. Paul Musselman, director of the Department of Evangelism for the National Council of Churches, said in a recent article, "The most compelling mission of the Church today is not in the far-off, least civilized corners of the globe. The biggest task lies right at the heart of urban civilization, in the tall towers and asphalt jungles of our cities. That is where the Church has failed." [25] Although the populations in the following cities have remained just about constant since 1945, he points out that during this time, New York City has lost more than 300 churches, Chicago has lost 150, Cleveland 72, and Detroit 63. Bryant George, associate director of the Urban Church Department of the United Presbyterian Church, gives a provocative commentary on the current situation, "Protestantism has marched fearlessly backward." [26] In many churches

---

[25] "Speaking Out: Churches Are Failing the Cities," *The Saturday Evening Post*, November 18, 1961, p. 10.
[26] *Ibid.*

the only ones who are being added to the membership are the children of the church members.

Also, in too many churches the members are attending the services of the church simply for their own spiritual enrichment. Of course, Bible study and worship in the church are important. But from one perspective these are means and not ends.[27] "The Early Church was like a beehive in reverse. There was much coming in and going out; but the coming in was to get renewed strength from fellowship, prayer, and the Breaking of Bread in order to take the precious Word of Salvation out to the uttermost parts of the earth." [28] Church members do not understand that a prime reason for their affiliation with the church and participation in its worship, study, and fellowships is that they might receive strength and motivation to "go out" into the world and give their witness.

It is the purpose and nature of God to seek sinful man. He is as a shepherd who leaves the ninety and nine to seek the one lost sheep. And he seeks the *last* one with the same loving concern and sense of urgency that he sought the first one. If this, then, is the purpose of God, it also is the task of the church.

Those who say that they are not interested in "numbers"; those who say they are interested in "quality" rather than "quantity" are simply deceiving themselves. The total emphasis of this book indicates that a premium is placed upon quality. But a person cannot be a "quality" Christian (so-called) unless he goes with Christ, and for Christ, out into the "highways and hedges" after the *last* one who needs Christ. It is the task of the church to go—and to keep going—so long as there is "one sheep" that is still lost. *The church that ministers only to its own is thereby failing to be the church.*

Small cell groups within the church may provide us with an important key in our search for an experiential religion.

---

[27] There is a sense in which the worship of God is its own end. However, if this is carried to the extreme it will lead to a monastic expression of religion and thus will vitiate the essential purpose of the Christian enterprise.

[28] John Heuss, *Our Christian Vocation* (Greenwich, Conn.: Seabury Press, 1955), pp. 10-11.

But if they do not lead the participants to reach men and women for Christ and for Bible study, then this very failure is evidence that they are not "quality" groups. If they seek only to build up their own spiritual lives, their lack of action indicates their failure to understand their purpose as instruments of God's redemptive purpose.

In seeking to reach the masses, the church must be careful to give witness to the whole gospel. That is, the church must not "water down" the gospel to make it more acceptable. The demands of the Christian life must be clearly enunciated. The response the people will be their own responsibility. If they refuse, then the church must keep on seeking. But the church must witness to all men.

Among many of the large religious groups in America today, this concern for "outreach" has not been a major emphasis. Why? Undoubtedly there have been many contributing causes. A principal one may be rooted in a certain theological perspective. Although there is common agreement among the major religious groups concerning man's sinful nature, there also seems to be confusion as to the condition of man and the destiny of man in light of that nature.

So incisive a thinker as James D. Smart illustrates this confusion (unless I misunderstand him). He is quite clear concerning the sinful nature of man. Man "is a sinner, imprisoned within himself by the power of sin dwelling in him." He was among the first in the field of religious education to condemn the view of salvation through ethical achievement, and he is quite clear in emphasizing the work of God in meeting man's need. "To be born of God cannot be man's achievement, but must be received by him as God's work in him and God's gift to him of his own life." [29]

However, Dr. Smart seems somewhat vague as to man's destiny if he is "out of Christ." In repudiating "certain evangelistic approaches" he says,

---

[29] *The Teaching Ministry of the Church* (Philadelphia: The Westminster Press, 1954), p. 160.

The prodigal, returning from the far country, heard from his father not the words, "You are a sinner," but the gracious words, "You are my son." Therefore, no matter how deeply a man has fallen into sin, our point of contact with him is our knowledge that beneath it all he is a child of God, and that, however broken his relationship with God may be, he cannot break God's relationship with him. He cannot deliver himself out of the hand of God.[30]

Dr. Smart goes on to say that the "old conversion" view "actually rests upon the assumption that until conversion man is by nature a sinner, in complete isolation from God, rather than a child of God, belonging to God, but with the order of his life distorted and perverted by sin."[31]

It is true that at this point Smart is discussing children who grow up in Christian homes, and this may make some difference in what he says and the way he says it. But earlier, in characterizing the "evangelistic" view, he says that no distinction is made between the four-year-old sinner, the fourteen-year-old sinner, and the twenty-four-year-old sinner. Those who hold the evangelistic view cannot accept this analysis. However, to make the issue more clear let us leave the child out of the picture and limit our consideration to the situation of the twenty-four-year-old sinner. In speaking of the parable of the prodigal son, Dr. Smart points out that the father still referred to him as "my son." But he does not make clear what the boy's condition was while this relationship was broken. It is true that every man is God's son by virtue of creation, but this does not mean that man stays in a "saving relationship" with the Father. In the parable the father referred to him as "my son" but he added: "which was *lost!*"

The question, then, is this: What is man's relationship with God, what is his destiny as he stands before God "with the order of his life distorted and perverted by sin"? Does it mean that the "son" is without "hope, and without God in the world" (Eph. 2:12)? Does it mean that this broken relationship is so

---

[30] *Ibid.*, p. 162.
[31] *Ibid.*, p. 163.

serious that the only way it can be restored is for the "son" to be "born again"? This is precisely what it means. This broken relationship is no mild break. Man "out of Christ" stands lost and condemned before God!

There are those who hold that in spite of the fact that man is a sinner, there will be a universal salvation. There are others who seem to feel that man will be given a "second chance." Still others seem to feel that although the nature of man is in disorder and only God can change it, a Lord of love and mercy will somehow cause things to come out all right in the end. They are quite reluctant to use such words as "lost," "condemned," "wrath of God," "without God and without hope in the world," "dead in trespasses and sins." These words are far too drastic for these people in separating those who are "saved" from those who are "lost." [32]

Thus, eschatology influences the emphasis which a church gives to this ministry of outreach. Admittedly many of the "last things" are shrouded in mystery so that there may be legitimate differences of opinion. Nevertheless, if God was willing to make the supreme sacrifice of his Son on the cross for man's redemption, is it not reasonable to suppose that the "final end" of man "out of Christ" (however it may be described) is desperate in nature? That desperate plight must match in some degree the costly grace that was provided for his salvation. Otherwise, God's act on the cross would have been unnecessary.

From God's perspective the "end of man out of Christ" was so serious in nature that he gave his Son that man might have eternal life. This is reason enough for the people of God to view the end of man with utmost seriousness. This seriousness must permeate the preaching and the teaching done by the church.

---

[32] Those who say they have the assurance of being "saved" are often accused of being guilty of the sin of pride because of this assurance. Such is not the case. We are keenly aware that although we have the assurance we are "in Christ," we are still sinners. We are also aware that it is only "by grace" that any of us are saved.

Another aspect of theology that has influenced the "out-reaching" emphasis of the church has been the "point" and "process" views of salvation. The Scriptures see salvation as both an event and a continuing experience, and they must be held in proper balance. Those who place an overemphasis on the process aspect of salvation tend not to be able to make a sufficient distinction between those who are "saved" and those who are "unsaved." [33] They emphasize the fact that salvation is fully consummated only beyond history, and in this life we live in the hope of being saved. Recognizing their own sinfulness, they hesitate to tell others that they are "lost" and need to be "saved." They tend to minister only to their own.

Although the emphasis on process has a solid foundation in the biblical doctrine of salvation, and the "saved" do continue to be sinners, nevertheless the Bible does speak of being "in Christ." It is not a question of whether these unreached people are as good as anyone else; the ultimate question is whether they are "in Christ"—a phrase which Deissmann says occurs 159 times in Paul's letters. He was convinced that there is a supreme difference between those who are "in Christ" and those who are not "in Christ." Thus, while the Christian may go out confessing that he, too, is a sinner, nevertheless he must still go out because he has a concern in his heart for the man who is not "in Christ."

One should not devise or hold a certain theological view just to develop in adherents a sense of urgency or to provide stimulus for action. But since this theological position has its basis in Scripture, it must be proclaimed with clarity, both to those in the church and to those in the world. Man's plight is desperate. There must be an outreach for the unreached! *There is reason for urgency in the work of the church!*

Motivation Underlying Concern

Now a word of caution is needed concerning the motive in reaching the unreached. Certainly the promotional methods

---

[33] The weakness in this overemphasis will be discussed on pp. 158-160.

used by the church should be consistent with a sound theology. Church and denominational leaders assume that the program and motivation are so based. But is this assumption valid so far as the average church member is concerned? In carrying out the church's program, does the average church member always do so from a genuinely Christian viewpoint and Christian motivation?

This is a fundamental problem. If people are busily engaged in carrying out many different acts which are related to the church but which have little or no Christian foundation or motivation, by such "busyness" we are leading them to deceive themselves into thinking that they are something they are not. In so doing we are merely developing a host of twentieth century Pharisees—active in religious work without being motivated by the Spirit of God.

Let us be specific: Here is a church which has set a numerical goal to be reached in one of its organizations; or here is a class which has divided itself into the "Reds" and the "Blues" to see who can enlist the most new members. Underlying these efforts is the assumption that if these people can be brought into the organization, they will be helped; there is also a general desire to "help" people. There is certainly merit in both the assumption and the desire. But we must ask: Is the concern of the average member based upon a deep yearning for the souls of men, and is he motivated by a genuinely Christian compassion? Too often his chief interest is with the contest to be won or the goal to be reached. Lacking Christian motivation, the activity, though related to the church, is thereby less than Christian.

This is not theological hairsplitting. It is a basic issue. It is a fundamental difference between Christianity and modern Pharisaism. In either case, the deeds or programs are similar if not the same. The difference is that while Christianity is concerned with deeds, it is not concerned primarily with deeds but with motive that prompts them. To the extent that our programs fail to be so motivated, to that extent they fail to be wholly Christian. To the extent that the "publicity" for our programs fails to emphasize this fact, to that extent we fail to emphasize the basically Christian aspect of our programs of the church.

The fact is our actions stem from a variety of motives, some of which are more worthy, and some of which are less worthy. We are concerned that the lost be won and the unreached be reached. Also we are often motivated to engage in an evangelistic effort, an enlargment campaign, or a visitation program from a sense of duty, a loyalty to the church's program, or a desire to increase enrolment. Our purpose here is not to sit in judgment upon any of these motives. It is simply a plea that we all, pastors and people, seek to lift our motives to the level that is Christian—after the spirit of Christ himself.

This does not at all mean that there will be a lessening of effort on our part to reach the unreached and to win the lost. There is a genuinely Christian theological basis for concern which, if rightly understood, if appropriated, and if acted upon, will lead to even increased effort on the part of Christians. To develop this attitude or this type of motivation on the part of people cannot be done overnight. It is a long range educational endeavor lasting throughout the life of the Christian. It is certainly not easy. It must permeate the curricular materials, the teaching, the preaching, the total program of the church.

It is really not difficult to get people to engage in some activity. We can devise a program, have a banquet, use certain techniques of publicity and promotion, and in a few weeks generate enough enthusiasm to cause people to undertake almost anything. But it is far easier to lead people to engage in action than it is to lead them to act from a Christian motivation. That is one reason it is so much easier to make Pharisees than it is to make Christians. Because it is easier, we must resist the temptation to be satisfied with mere activity. Neither must we deceive ourselves into thinking that because we get the activity, the proper motivation is also present. There is a motivation for action. This is the goal toward which we must strive.

Is Extrinsic Motivation Ever Justified?

To be fair, we must also look at the other side of this issue. Is it ever legitimate for church leaders to use extrinsic, i.e., nonspiritual, motivation in stimulating Christians to engage in Christian pursuits? Though it may seem strange in light of what has just been said, the answer is "yes." This answer also has its theological foundation. The Christian is sinner as well as saint. Because the Christian remains a sinner, it is not only legitimate but necessary to rely, at times, upon extrinsic motivation. If I seem to be speaking with a "split tongue," it is precisely because the Christian is a split being, sinner and saint, that this is necessary. Thus, so eminent a Christian as the apostle Paul had to cry, "What I would, that do I not; but what I hate, that do I" (Rom. 7:15).

In motivating the Christian we cannot deal with him as though he were wholly saint. At no part of his life does he ever act from completely Christian motivations. Shall we say then, Do not act unless you act from a purely Christian motive? No! We are Christians striving toward perfection but we remain sinners. It is important, however, that the Christian be aware of the fact that he acts—even in his good acts—on the basis of mixed motives, some of which are less worthy than others. Nevertheless, as Cherbonnier suggests, let him go ahead and act. Good may come from it. But let him confess his mixed motives and ask God's forgiveness. "A Christian does good works, then, not in a spirit of 'what a good boy am I,' but rather, 'Lord, have mercy—I had to do it more from duty than from *agape.'* " [34]

How, then, shall we solve our dilemma? Since man is sinner, it seems that we are forced to rely, in part at least, upon ex-

---

[34] E. LaB. Cherbonnier, *Hardness of Heart* (Garden City, N. Y.: Doubleday & Co., Inc., 1955), p. 140.

trinsic motivation. Yet to use extrinsic motivation may lead to Pharisaism. The problem is not easy to solve. Two fundamental points indicate the fine line which the leadership of the church must walk. First, church leaders must understand that when they use extrinsic motivation to stimulate to action, they are dealing with Christians as sinners. When they rely upon spiritual motivation they are dealing with them as saints. Although it is necessary to deal with Christians as sinners, we should strive always toward developing them so that increasingly we might deal with them as saints.

Second, the more the church emphasizes and relies upon extrinsic motivation for the promotion of its work, the greater will be the tendency toward externalism and institutionalism in religion. The more the church utilizes and magnifies spiritual motives, the more religion will tend to be experiential. This line is so fine and is so difficult to walk that the church throughout history has tended to "fall off" on the side of institutionalism.

9

Authentic Faith and an Approach to Evangelism

If the nature of man is such that in his "natural" condition he is alienated from God, then the fundamental need of man is to be brought into a saving relationship with God. Since man cannot solve his human predicament within himself, his salvation must come from a source outside himself. God has acted uniquely in Jesus Christ in behalf of sinful man; thus man must come into a saving relationship with God through Christ. What is the nature of this saving relationship, and what approach to evangelism must the church take in light of the nature of this relationship?

Preliminary Problems

To see as clearly as is possible, to understand as fully as possible is the divine imperative placed upon us. Immediately, however, we face several problems. First of all, we are dealing with an area in which it is God who works, and thus it defies complete analysis by rational processes. Finite minds cannot comprehend fully the work of the infinite God.

In the second place, we confront a problem that might be labeled "verbalism." In its essence, the Christian faith consists of a relationship between God and man through Christ. It is a relationship so intimate and vital that Jesus likened it to a vine and its branches. To be genuine, this relationship must be of such dynamic quality that God infuses the life of the individual with his transforming grace. It is of such a radical quality that Jesus spoke of it as being "born again." In seeking to lead an individual into this relationship, from the human perspective, we must rely largely upon words, either spoken or written. The danger of verbalism is that the individual may learn the words that describe this experience, give his affirmation to these words, but never genuinely enter into this relationship with God.

Third, we face a semantic problem. Communication is not simply a process of taking meaning out of words; it is also the process of putting meaning into words. When an individual hears a spoken word or reads a written word, he does not so much take the meaning of the speaker or writer out of the word as he puts his own meaning into the word. For example, a brilliant scientist may use the term "nuclear physics." When I read these words, I do not see in them the wealth of meaning they have for the scientist. Thus, when an individual reads or hears. "Whosoever believeth in him should not perish" or "Believe on the Lord Jesus Christ, and thou shalt be saved," he does not primarily take out of these words the meaning of Jesus or Paul; he puts his own meaning into the words. He may put only a rather shallow, superficial meaning into them.

Finally, one's view of the nature and meaning of the Christian life inevitably influences one's view of how a person enters the Christian life. On the one hand, if religious groups view the Christian life as something simple and relatively easy, that is, in terms of living a good moral life and attending the meetings of the church, they tend to view salvation or how one becomes a Christian in simple, relatively easy terms. On the other hand, if the Christian life means that the individual has embarked on a mission for God in the world, committing himself to do the will of God even against worldly opposition, then this life is not entered on the basis of a shallow profession or superficial experience.

Certain passages in the New Testament seem to indicate that it is quite easy to become a Christian. "Whosoever shall not receive the kingdom of God as a little child, he shall not enter therein" (Mark 10:15). Other passages seem to indicate that it is quite difficult. "Whosoever he be of you that forsaketh not all that he hath, he cannot be my disciple" (Luke 14:33). How, then, does one enter the Christian life? For the church to answer this question with care and accuracy in light of the teaching of the New Testament is one of its most important tasks. The answer will largely determine the church's approach to evangelism.

Current Weaknesses

Through the years Southern Baptists have been an evangelistic people. Our efforts have been blessed with singular success. We have had phenomenal numerical growth. This emphasis on evangelism must never slacken. Rather, we need even greater emphasis on winning the lost to Christ. Yet at the risk of being misunderstood, it is necessary to point out what seem to be two basic weaknesses in our present approach to evangelism.

Our first weakness lies in the fact that we have tended to place primary emphasis upon the initial decision for Christ and have failed to emphasize adequately the development of Christian personality and character. The second weakness is related to the first yet different. In leading people to make a "decision for Christ," we too often have been content with leading them into a shallow profession or superficial experience. We have not understood adequately, nor have we led the potential convert to understand adequately the nature of the saving relationship. We have taught and preached that a person was saved by grace, but we have not reflected the biblical teachings concerning "costly grace."

Undoubtedly there are many reasons for this present emphasis. Let us consider four. First, our doctrine of man has led us to be deeply conscious of man's lost condition, and in our zeal to have him saved we have been content with leading him to take only the initial step with Christ, We have not been sufficiently concerned about the depth and quality of this relationship.

A second reason for our present emphasis is our view of salvation. Regardless of our theological position, Southern Baptists have appeared to feel that if we could get a man out of his lost condition and into the kingdom, then the "big job" was done. The difficulty with this position is that it tends to make salvation too mechanical, as scarcely more than walking down the aisle and giving the preacher one's hand. The saving relationship of Christ with the convert is in no wise mechanical; rather it is a "vine-branch" relationship so real that life and power flow from the one to the other. The spiritual implications of the conversion experience are so great and far-reaching that the new convert is not even conscious of all of them at the time of his initial experience with Christ. Therefore, the "big job" is not over at the time of conversion. It has only begun.

A third reason for our lack of emphasis upon the responsibility to develop functioning Christians is the assumption that the new convert will automatically live the Christian life if he is "really saved" and that he will automatically develop Christian character. This assumption has no basis in fact. It is true that some lives have been remarkably transformed at the time of the conversion experience. However, moral and ethical changes take place in a person's life only in those areas in which there is true conviction of sin. The Holy Spirit continues his work of conviction and growth throughout the life of the believer, but Christian character does not come automatically, either at conversion or afterward.

Undoubtedly a fourth reason is the negative reaction to the "salvation by works" doctrine of those who emphasized the "social gospel" almost to the exclusion of personal redemption. Some seem to fear that if any strong emphasis is given to the kind of life a Christian must live, it might tend to hide the fact that salvation is by faith alone. Others fear that if special attention is given the social aspects of the gospel, church members might forget that each individual is accountable before God and salvation comes only by individual choice.

Whatever the reasons for the present emphasis, the weaknesses are everywhere apparent. In our desire to magnify evangelism we have, in reality, hindered the development of an adequate, progressive evangelistic program. In recent years approximately five thousand Southern Baptist churches have failed to report a single convert for the entire year. Statistically, it takes more than twenty Southern Baptists an entire year to win one person to Christ. With all our emphasis on evangelism, why does this condition exist? The answer is simple. The only way to have a great evangelistic program is to develop church members who themselves are evangelists. But this cannot be done while the major emphasis is upon leading the individual to have only an initial experience with Christ. Undeveloped Christians do not become fervent evangelists!

Therefore, religious leaders must face realistically the question: What is involved in a genuine saving relationship? This is a pertinent problem because next Sunday, and all the weeks following, evangelists, pastors, Sunday school teachers, and other Christians will be seeking to lead people toward this saving encounter with God. What do we need to lead them to understand is involved? What demands concerning life shall we press upon them? How high must our standards be to meet the New Testament's challenge of experiential religion? What degree of commitment of life shall we ask them to make?

Some one may ask: "Cannot God save a person without his knowing the demands upon his life? After all, one is saved not by knowledge but by grace through faith. It is fundamentally a relationship. None of us knows fully the demands of Christ upon our lives." This brings us back to the original question: What constitutes authentic faith?

The Gift of God

Two New Testament passages outline clearly the two sides of the issue being considered.

Ephesians 2:8-9: "By grace are ye saved through faith; and that not of yourselves: it is the gift of God: not of works, lest any man should boast." Verse 10 is almost always left out by those who quote this passage: "For we are his workmanship, created in Christ Jesus unto good works, which God hath before ordained that we should walk in them."

James 2:14,19-20: "What doth it profit, my brethren, though a man say he hath faith, and have not works? can faith save him? . . . Thou believest that there is one God; thou doest well: the devils also believe, and tremble. But wilt thou know, O vain man, that faith without works is dead?"

One passage emphasizes that salvation is not only the work of God, it is the gift of God. The emphasis here is on grace. The other passage considers the depth and quality of faith that is authentic faith. To the first emphasis we now turn our attention.

In the first passage four points should be noted. *First*, this saving relationship is based upon encounter with the living God. It is essentially relational in nature. This divine-human encounter must be deep and dynamic because of its decisive nature. Certainly there is growth that leads up to this encounter, and growth follows it. But the encounter itself is decisive in nature. The individual must be aware of who he is and who God is. He must be aware of the nature of the life to which he is being called and of the implications of the decision which he is making. It is difficult to describe the nature of this decision without implying that it is always cataclysmic in nature. Such is not intended. It does not have to be cataclysmic. If proper growth has preceded the decision, it may be made in utter quietness. However, this does not change the depth, the quality, or the decisiveness of the encounter.

Second, and perhaps most fundamental, salvation is always a gift. There is nothing that man can do to earn, merit, or deserve it. As Baillie says, "it is all of God." While salvation involves a changed life, no righteousness which man may possess can in any way contribute to his salvation. Otherwise, man would become proud of his righteousness and thus would remain guilty. The fact that salvation is a gift hits man at the point it hurts most—his pride—his complete inability to contribute in any way to his salvation. Jesus was never more piercing than in his condemnation of self-righteousness as in the parable of the Pharisee and the publican (Luke 18:9-14). Nor does man contribute to his salvation by his awareness of sin. If this were the case, he would become proud of his awareness of sin and would portray the parable of the Pharisee and the publican in reverse. Thus, man would cry, "I thank thee that I am not as this Pharisee. I am aware of my sin!" Salvation is wholly gift. It is "by grace through faith."

The *third* point may seem to contradict what has just been said. Although salvation is wholly gift, man's decision determines his destiny. Some might say that if man's decision determines his destiny, then he could become proud of his decision and thus would remain guilty. No. Man's decision does not contribute to his salvation; his decision is only the acceptance of the salvation which is given by God.

Fourth, that grace which is the basis of salvation, wholly the work of God and the gift of God, is a costly grace. "It is costly, both because it cost Jesus Christ his life's blood to make it effective, and further because it costs us a complete giving up of ourselves." [1] It is here that too many churches have been guilty of one of their most serious misinterpretations of a biblical teaching. In the effort to magnify the work of God, the love of God, the mercy of God, many churches have developed the perverted view of "cheap grace," as Bonhoeffer calls it. Seemingly they have reasoned that since salvation is by grace and all that man has to do is "have faith," we will magnify the work if we emphasize his "grace." If we emphasize the kind of life that is required, this will imply that salvation is by works. *Thus, no adequate emphasis has been placed on the kind and quality of life that must be lived under grace.*

The average church member also reasons on the basis of what he has heard preached and taught in the church: "Our God is a gracious God. He is 'not willing that any should perish.' All I have to do is 'believe,' and I do believe, so all must be well with me. It's up to God to save me." How easy

---

[1] Rutenber, *op. cit.*, pp. 169-170.

it is to use words that are so close to the truth and yet be so far from the truth! "It is under the influence of this kind of 'grace' that the world has been made 'Christian,' but at the cost of secularizing the Christian religion as never before."[2]

Martin Luther, who rediscovered the biblical emphasis on salvation by faith and made it the basis of the Reformation, never understood this to involve a cheap grace. Luther describes the release he felt when he discovered that man was justified by faith alone. This

experience taught him that this grace had cost him his very life, and must continue to cost him the same price day by day. . . . When he spoke of grace, Luther always implied as a corollary that it cost him his own life, the life which was now for the first time subjected to the absolute obedience of Christ. Only so could he speak of grace.[3]

The warning of Dietrich Bonhoeffer to his own Lutheran people, should be a warning to all evangelical churches. He wrote in 1937 in Hitler's Germany that Luther's doctrine of justification by grace had been paid the highest honors in the church.

Everywhere Luther's formula has been repeated, but its truth perverted into self-deception. So long as our Church holds the correct doctrine of justification, there is no doubt whatever that she is a justified Church! So they said, thinking that we must vindicate our Lutheran heritage by making this grace available on the cheapest and easiest terms. . . . The result was that a nation became Christian and Lutheran, but at the cost of true discipleship. The price it was called upon to pay was all too cheap. Cheap grace has won the day. But do we also realize that this cheap grace has turned back upon us like a boomerang? The price we are having to pay today in the shape of the collapse of the organized church is only the inevitable consequence of our policy of making grace available to all at too low a cost. . . . Cheap grace has turned out to be utterly merciless to our Evangelical Church.[4]

This is still the sin of the church. It is one of the major factors leading to externalism in religion, and thus to institutionalism.

---

[2] Bonhoeffer, *op. cit.*, p. 42.
[3] *Ibid.*, p. 41.
[4] *Ibid.*, p. 45.

Costly grace is still grace—but it is costly. Evangelism as practiced by the church, if it is to be faithful to the New Testament, must emphasize the fact of costly grace. It not only cost the life of the Son of God, but it will also cost the believer his own life.

Authentic Faith

The term "authentic faith" is used here to designate that faith often referred to as "saving faith." This term "saving faith," while descriptive, is not technically accurate. It implies that it is "faith," or man's act, that saves; in reality it is God who saves "through faith." It tends to make salvation anthropocentric. But salvation is theocentric, and "authentic faith" indicates the quality of the faith that is involved in the relationship in which God works his divine work of salvation.

The passage from James emphasizes the nature of faith: "Faith without works is dead." What is involved in authentic faith? This is a difficult and delicate area because we are still where God works. But we must see the answer clearly if we are to practice true evangelism.

With his newly discovered emphasis on justification by faith Martin Luther felt that the book of James was a "right strawey epistle." Some scholars say that James was seeking to combine Christianity with legalistic Judaism. Others see direct conflict between the positions of Paul and of James. Actually, there is no essential conflict between these two. Paul was not against works, as Ephesians 2:10 clearly shows, and James was not against faith. They were looking at salvation from two different viewpoints. In describing the work of salvation, Paul was magnifying the power of God—that it is God's power and God's power alone that can save an individual. James, looking at salvation from the viewpoint of man, was emphasizing the human manifestation of the power of God having worked in man. He shows us how a genuine faith acts. He said in effect, "Authentic faith produces life according to the will of God, while a life contrary to the will of God denies faith in God."

The faith that is merely a pious intellectual assent to a creed or formula, without corresponding works, is dead. Such faith without works is just as unable to save a person as a few pious words are unable to clothe a naked man or to feed a hungry man (2:15). The only way we can tell genuine saving faith is by its fruit. One may hold in his hand a kernel of corn. A chemist can analyze its component parts and make one exactly like it. Looking at the two seeds we cannot tell the difference. But there is a very real difference. The one the chemist made is dead, lifeless, worthless. The other has life and life-giving power. The only way we can tell the difference is to plant the two seeds. The one will sprout and produce fruit; the other will remain in the ground. It is dead.

If our faith produces fruit—Godlike works—then it is genuine faith. If it does not produce Godlike living, then that faith is inadequate, worthless, dead. Like the chemist's seed, it never had life in the first place. We must lead people to see clearly that this Godlike living is involved in authentic faith and lead them to accept Christ on the basis of this demand. For "by their fruits ye shall know them" (Matt. 7:20).

Elements Involved in Authentic Faith

In describing authentic faith more fully, we note three elements that must be present if the faith is truly authentic. *First,* authentic faith requires a response that involves the totality of one's being. In this relationship man cannot respond with his intellect alone, or with his emotions alone, or with his will alone, or with any other part of his life—alone. This does not mean that every area and relationship of life is automatically changed in this response. Both experience and the Bible indicate that this is not true. But it does mean that man is a unity, and when he responds to Christ, he responds with his "essential self" (not a "self" in isolation but a "self" in relationship). "Nothing less than this total re-creation of the soul and of its world will pass for Christian conversion. To have confidence in aught else, however sanctioned by ancient custom or prized by conventional religion, is to delude oneself." [5] God could have required nothing that would have been so all-inclusive in its demand as that of faith. It requires a response of the totality of one's being.

Second, authentic faith involves a response in which one surrenders his life to the sovereignty of God. This emphasis on the sovereignty of God was minimized during the first third of the twentieth century. The emphasis then was on the freedom of man, the creativity of man, and the democratic ideal. George Albert Coe phrased the aim of religious education in terms of the "democracy of God." "The aim of Christian education becomes this: *Growth of the young toward and into mature and efficient devotion to the democracy of God, and happy self-realization therein.*" [6] Harrison Elliott raised serious objections to the view that the way to be Christian is "for man to give up his attempts to find his own way and yield completely to the sovereign and loving reign of God." It is through the assertion of man's will that growth takes place. Thus "it would seem as if the God of the universe had taken that risk in endowing man with the capacities which made his rebellion against absolute authority possible, and that he expected man to exercise rather than surrender his freedom." [7]

Yet complete surrender to the sovereignty of God is precisely the demand that God makes. Those who seek to eliminate "this 'pricking' element of absolute claim," says Farmer, would thus eliminate "that which, more than anything else, throws into the sharpest relief the distinctive essence of the . . . living touch of God upon the human spirit." [8] The Christian is not allowed the luxury of following his own natural desires nor in a given situation is he allowed the privilege of holding

[5] R. E. O. White, *Into the Same Image* (Nashville: Broadman Press, 1957), p. 17.

[6] *A Social Theory of Religious Education,* p. 55.

[7] *Can Religious Education Be Christian?* (New York: The Macmillan Company, 1940), pp. 152, 156.

[8] H. H. Farmer, *Revelation and Religion* (London: Nisbet & Co., Ltd., 1954), p. 142.

the purely "human" attitude. The Christian is under the sovereignty of another. He is not his own. He has been bought with a price. He can only ask, "What is the will of God?" By this he is bound.

If a fundamental expression of the Christian life is doing the will of God on earth regardless of the cost to the believer, then this submission to the sovereignty of God must be present in a "saving" relationship with Christ. It is only after the individual has made a surrender in which the "natural man" is brought under the sovereignty of God that the individual ever becomes willing to undertake such things as loving his enemies or even his neighbor as himself. Surrender to the sovereignty of God is essential to experiential religion. When this emphasis is in any way lessened, religion tends to become superficial. Matching man's surrender is his assurance that he can rely completely upon God as the "source and guarantee of man's final security and good." [9]

Having a shallow view of the conversion experience, most churches seem content with leading their members to commit themselves to moralisms such as "being good." Because of the shallowness of the average member's relationship with Christ, he is neither ready nor willing to meet the demands of the Christian life in any of its deeper and more fundamental aspects. He may readily confess that he "ought" to do these things, but when an issue comes up involving sacrifice or personal ostracism, the church member can usually justify his silence or compromise. Of course, he has a certain "faith" in Christ, but it is not the kind that would lead him to stake his social standing on the proposition that Christ's way is the right way. Thus, personal sacrifice remains merely a point in a sermon, agreed to by all but rarely lived by.

Third, authentic faith involves a response in which the individual gives himself to be an instrument of God's redemptive purpose. Here is no "cheap grace" that has little or no effect upon the life of man. Here is grace that calls man to a mission.

---

[9] *Ibid.,* p. 138.

And it is in terms of this mission that man must respond. "Conversion," says Gabriel Marcel, "is the act by which man is called to become a witness." [10] Trueblood puts it bluntly, "A faith which a person is not trying to share is not genuine." [11]

The doctrine of election gives in clear and unmistakable terms the reason God is calling to himself a "new Israel." God is engaged in a redemptive mission in the world and he is calling to himself "a people" to join with him in this mission. Thus when the individual unites with God through Christ in a saving relationship, the individual's response to God must be in terms of that for which he was called. That is, if God calls the individual to one thing and the individual, misunderstanding the nature of this call, commits himself to something else, then the relationship that ensues is not sound or necessarily saving.

A homely illustration might throw light on this point. One friend meets another and says, "There is something important going on down at Fourth and Broadway. Come and share it with me." The second friend says, "Thanks, I'll be delighted to accept your invitation." The second person knows that there is a large hotel at Fourth and Broadway, and he has heard that they are having a banquet there with excellent food and entertainment. When they arrive, however, an Army recruitment booth has been set up in front of the hotel, and his friend wants him to enlist for war. The second friend could only plead. "Excuse me! I didn't know this was what you had in mind!" He had responded to the "banquet" idea but not to the army. Thus, his initial commitment or response, regardless of how sincere and genuine it may have been when he made it, was not sound because that to which he had committed himself was different from that to which he was invited.

This homely example may not be too far off, at that. Some respond to the invitation of God as though he was inviting them to a feast, an eternal party in heaven, when in reality he is inviting them to enlist for war.

---

[10] *The Mystery of Being* (London: The Harvill Press, Ltd., 1951), II, 133.

[11] *The Company of the Committed*, p. 59.

One of the most surprising facts about the early Church was its fundamental similarity to a military band. . . . The notion of enlisting Church members as recruits sounds very strange to modern ears. This reaction tells us something significant about the Church of the twentieth century; it tells us how far we have drifted.[12]

God's invitation is for volunteers who are willing to give their lives to be instruments for accomplishing his redemptive purpose in the world. When an individual responds to the "big social" idea, then his commitment is not sound, regardless of how sincere it may be.

Yet it would probably be accurate to say that the fundamental motive that lies at the center of the average church member's "decision for Christ" is the desire to escape the "horrors of hell" and share in the "joys of heaven." Of course, man lives in the hope of eternal life. This is no small part of the Christian experience. It is a worthy and valid hope. But when the hope of heaven constitutes the whole of one's religious experience, there is reason to question whether he has entered into a genuine saving relationship. E. Stanley Jones speaks to this point when he says,

escaping hell and getting to heaven . . . is involved in conversion, but if it is made the end in view of conversion it will . . . let you down. If you pursue heaven as the goal, it will elude you. If you should pursue heaven as a goal, when you got it you wouldn't be fit for it, for you had the wrong motive in trying to get it. Heaven is a by-product and not the goal or end.[13]

P. T. Forsyth expresses the same point of view: "Our Lord did not come to save souls, or to gather devout groups, or even to found churches, but so to save souls and found churches as to make Christian nations and thus change society to the Kingdom of God." [14]

Thus in seeking to understand the nature of authentic faith, it might be said that salvation is not and, by its nature, cannot

[12] *Ibid.*, pp. 30-31.
[13] *Conversion* (New York: Abingdon Press, 1959), p. 240.
[14] As quoted in Miller, *op. cit.*, p. 50.

be, only an end which the individual seeks. "According to Matt. v. 15 and the rest of the New Testament, a lamp kindled by God is not lit for itself but for all who are in the house." [15] If an individual wants only to receive forgiveness of sins and the hope of heaven, his desire is no better or higher than that of the Jews of Jesus' day, who at the feeding of the five thousand also desired "what Jesus had to offer," but who, when a more complete explanation of the implications of this relationship was given, turned and walked no more with him.

Man is saved when he comes into a relationship with God in which he recognizes that only God can be God in his life and in the life of every man. It is a relationship in which he accepts God's way in Christ as the only way in his life and in the life of every man. On this basis he surrenders to the lordship of Christ in his life and joins in his mission to accomplish the redemptive purpose of God in the life of every man. As he gives himself to this mission, he "loses his life" and thus "finds his life"; that is, is saved.

Note that Jesus did not say, "He that loses his life *to try to find life* shall find it." This is selfish at the core. Rather, Jesus said, "He that loseth his life *for my sake* shall find it" (Matt. 10:39;16:25). Thus man is saved, not primarily because he seeks salvation as an end in itself, but rather salvation comes because one has entered into a relationship with Christ in which he loses his own life in joining with Jesus in his redemptive mission. Salvation always comes to an individual on its way to someone else.

All of what God does *in* us and *for* us is in order that he may do things *through* us for the sake of our fellowmen. . . . God cannot be "used" for our purposes at all. When we become Christians, we offer ourselves to be used for Christ's purposes.[16]

Thus the question which ministers traditionally ask people, "Do you want to be saved?" is largely irrelevant. The person

---

[15] Karl Barth, *The Teaching of the Church Regarding Baptism,* trans. Ernest A. Payne (London: S.C.M. Press, 1948), p. 31.

[16] Rutenber, *op. cit.,* pp. 68, 144.

who does not want to be saved, who does not want forgiveness instead of condemnation, who does not want life instead of death, is foolish. Rather, we need to ask the potential convert the question, "Do you believe so strongly that God's way is the only way that you are willing to give your life to making his way become a reality in the world and in the life of every man, no matter what the cost?"

The man or woman who will answer this question with life itself has authentic faith. If the essence of God's call is a call to a mission, then no genuine relationship can be consummated unless it is culminated in terms of this call. If this is the purpose for which God is calling men, then must not man respond in terms of that purpose?

Does not Christ's dealing with the Pharisees give a frightening warning as to what happens when the central purpose of God's election is in any way misunderstood or lost? The Pharisees had a "faith in God." They were a very religious people, and it may be assumed that they had a measure of sincerity in their understanding and expression of religion. Their sin was not only that they did not "recognize" that Jesus was the divine Son of God. Their sin was that they did not understand or accept the redemptive purpose that God was seeking to carry out through his Son and through them. This is the precise point of the "elder brother" in the parable of the prodigal son. For this reason they were rejected—lost. Therefore, "faith" includes the giving of oneself to be an instrument of God's redemptive purpose in the world for this is precisely that for which the individual is being called. Not to respond to this mission is to respond to something other than the call of God![17]

Yet through the years too many churches have come to feel that this radical call is too difficult for the masses. They have

---

[17] Although the wide variety of individual differences makes any dogmatic statement impossible, there is a real question whether the average child six to eight years old can have any adequate comprehension of what is involved for life in uniting with God in his redemptive purpose. Samuel Southard has an excellent chapter on "The Evangelism of Children," in *Pastoral Evangelism* (Nashville: Broadman Press, 1962), pp. 83-104.

found that if the "bars are lowered," more people can be "brought in," and they assume a God of grace will forgive their sins. At least this seems to be the way we have rationalized our present approach to evangelism. However, the people of God and their leaders stand under the judgment of God concerning their faithfulness (1 Cor. 4:2). First, they stand under judgment for their faithfulness in giving their witness to the world and in the world. Second, they stand under judgment concerning the nature of the gospel to which they give witness. They must declare the true gospel in the fulness of its demands. If the church is going to seek an experiential faith, this emphasis on the radical nature of the call of God and the necessity of man's radical response to this call must be kept in clear focus. History indicates that a loss or a minimizing of this emphasis leads to externalism in religion.

If this is what is involved in authentic faith, then this radical demand must be clearly and fully taught in the church's approach to evangelism. If, in so doing, the number of "converts" declines, the church must have sufficient strength to resist the temptation to bow to the pressure of the "success" psychology that has become dominant in our churches today. The church must also resist the unbiblical view that a loving God will save just on the basis of a "profession." Salvation is a relationship. God saves by grace through faith. But this faith involves a response of the totality of one's being in which the individual surrenders himself to the sovereignty of God and gives himself as an instrument of God's redemptive purpose. The church must always remember that it is this to which and for which the individual is called by God.

Let us emphasize the fact again that salvation is wholly by grace. We are not proclaiming a salvation by works. The man who understands the mission to which God is calling him, who seeks to be an instrument of God's redemptive purpose, who always tries to discover and express the will of God in his life relationships, this man is still a sinner. He recognizes himself as sinner. The man thus closely related to God will probably be more aware of his sinfulness than others will be. He will cry with the apostle Paul, "I am the chief of sinners." It is only by the infinite mercy and grace of God that anyone can be saved. But it is not a "cheap grace." The essential nature of the Christian life (as understood in terms of the doctrine of election, the priesthood of believers, and the concept of the will of God) indicates that the three factors just presented inhere in the "vine-branch" relationship; that is, in the saving relationship.

Understanding Before Decision

In the salvation relationship it is the quality of relationship and the depth of commitment that are truly decisive. It is impossible for a person to have complete understanding of what this new relationship involves. The young couple who get married do not know all that is involved in their new relationship, but their commitment to each other prepares them to "weather the storms" that come. Even the disciples of Jesus did not understand all that was involved in his purpose. Yet they had a quality of relationship with him and a depth of commitment to him that led them to accept the new insights and difficult tasks as they came.

Because the saving relationship is an intelligent relationship, however, the individual must have some understanding before he makes his "decision for Christ." It will be primarily in two areas: (1) understanding the nature of the saving relationship, and (2) understanding the nature of the Christian life. These will now be considered in order.

If what has been said in the preceding section has any basis in the teachings of the New Testament, it is necessary for the individual to have—to some degree—an understanding of the nature of the relationship into which he is entering. The key phrase here is "to some degree." How much is it necessary for an individual to understand in order for him to enter into an intelligent and genuine relationship with God? Here there will be wide and honest differences of opinion. No one would presume to say how much a person must "know" in order to be saved. Just understanding the biblical view of salvation does not necessarily lead to salvation. "Faith is not something fundamentally intellectual; its vitality lies in the fact that it is interpersonal and relational." [18] Some understanding, however, is necessary for this commitment to be intelligent and genuine. Without it, a person's commitment may be to something other than the call of God as revealed in the Scriptures.

Again a human relationship might throw some light on the point under consideration. An adult male may say, "Marry me," to a small girl who is too young to comprehend the nature and demands of the marriage relationship. She may reply, "I will," and she may have a genuine fondness for the man, but this does not constitute an adequate basis for true marriage. If the man tried to carry through with such a marriage, the courts would prohibit it on the basis of the child's age. She was not sufficiently mature to understand the meaning of the relationship. Marriage in its essence is a relationship—a *union* of two beings. It is impossible for this union to take place if one of the individuals does not understand its nature and demands.

No one can state precisely "how much'" a person should know before he is "ready" to enter either the marriage relationship or a saving relationship with God. However, in light of the teachings of the Scriptures and in light of our analysis of recent trends, we seem to have erred seriously in not insisting that the individual have a clear understanding of the saving relationship before baptizing him and receiving him into church membership.

The second area of understanding has to do with the nature and demands of the Christian life. In talking with the prospective convert we emphasize, and rightly so, that he must be "born again." But we seldom give him any idea of what the "born-again life" is like. We say that when an individual becomes a Christian he is a "new creature." Too often we do not explain how new this "new creature" is to be. Of course, we assume that the individual will learn what is involved in the

[48] Miller, *op. cit.*, p. 86.

Christian life after he becomes a church member. After all, we reason, we cannot lead the potential convert to know *all* that is involved in the Christian life before he makes his decision. Certainly, that is true. But to be honest with the individual who is about to make a momentous decision and to be true to the teachings of the New Testament, are we not obligated to lead him to face frankly, at least in general (and whenever possible, specifically, cf. Luke 3:10-14), the implications of the Christian way of life?

When we face this question realistically, we run into a practical, and perhaps, a theological problem. On the one hand, when we are seeking to lead a lost person to Christ, we have an intense desire for him to make the decision. At best, it is a difficult decision. If we talk too much about the implications of the Christian way for his life, the decision would be even more difficult. In our deep concern for him we want to make it as easy as possible for him. No unnecessary obstacle should bar the way. After all, it is God, and God alone, who does the saving. All the individual has to do, or can do, is respond in faith. The individual cannot save himself by his works. It is only by the grace of God that any of us—the best and the worst alike—are saved.

Unquestionably, much of the convert's instruction and understanding must come after the conversion experience. But we must go to Jesus for our pattern. He yearned for the lost to be saved. That was his purpose for coming into the world. But he wanted each believer to understand whom he was accepting and what was involved in this acceptance. For example, there was the experience of the feeding of the five thousand. After Jesus fed this multitude, they clamored to make him king. But the next day when he gave the spiritual interpretation of the "bread of life," his teaching proved an obstacle to the faith of many. "Many therefore of his disciples, when they had heard this, said, This is an hard saying; who can hear it? . . . From that time many of his disciples went back, and walked no more with him" (John 6:60-66). What a tragedy to lose this

large group of followers. Could not this instruction involving
"demand" have waited until after "church membership"?
Evidently not. Jesus insisted that they understand who he was
and what he was inviting them to do *before* they made their
final decision.

Again a rich young ruler came inquiring of Jesus what he
must do to inherit eternal life. After referring him to the Commandments and receiving the reply that the Commandments
had been kept, Jesus said, "Yet lackest thou one thing: sell
all that thou hast, and distribute unto the poor, and thou shalt
have treasure in heaven: and come, follow me. And when he
heard this, he was very sorrowful: for he was very rich"
(Luke 18:22-23).

Who of us, as we read this account, has not felt pangs of
regret, not only because the young ruler failed to enter the
kingdom, but also because of what he could have meant to the
Christian movement? Was this not an extreme demand made
upon the young inquirer as a condition for inheriting eternal
life? Could not this instruction have waited until after his
commitment? The young man had so much in his favor. He
kept the Commandments; evidently, he was morally clean; he
was a man of means; he was a person of influence; he was an
honest inquirer. In spite of all of this, Jesus did not make it
"easy" for him to become a Christian. He insisted that the
inquirer understand what was involved—for his personal life
—in following him, *before* he made his decision.

These are not isolated incidents in the experience of Jesus,
picked to prove a point. Throughout his ministry he was constantly urging those who would be his disciples (learners) to
count the cost of being his followers.

And there went great multitudes with him: and he turned, and said
unto them, If any man come to me, and hate not his father, and
mother, and wife, and children, and brethren, and sisters, yea, and
his own life also, he cannot be my disciple. . . . For which of you,
intending to build a tower, sitteth not down first, and counteth the
cost, whether he have sufficient to finish it? . . . Or what king, going

to make war against another king, sitteth not down first, and consulteth whether he be able with ten thousand to meet him that cometh against him with twenty thousand? . . . So likewise, whosoever he be of you that forsaketh not all that he hath, he cannot be my disciple (Luke 14:25-33).

On another occasion "he said to them all, If any man will come after me, let him deny himself, and take up his cross daily, and follow me. For whosoever will save his life shall lose it: but whosoever will lose his life for my sake, the same shall save it" (Luke 9:23-24).

Following Jesus is not easy. The implications of the conversion experience are life-changing! It is a new birth! The individual becomes a new creature! Evidently, Jesus wanted the individual to understand this and to count the cost of the experience to his daily life before he made his decision.

As we face the two sides of this problem, we are met with a real difficulty. On the one hand, in our desire to see people saved, we would not place one unnecessary obstacle in their way to hinder their acceptance, realizing that salvation is wholly by grace through faith. On the other hand, there is the emphasis of Jesus that the individual understand what is involved in following him. In our approach to evangelism we are under obligation to follow the New Testament pattern, not personal preferences.

If being Christian means accepting God's mission in the world, if it means engaging in a ministry which must be performed in the world, if it means coming into conflict with the world as one gives his witness to God, if it may lead to suffering and a cross, then all this should be clearly understood and accepted by the individual *before* he makes his decision. In the truly Christian life there is a price to be paid, and the individual must carefully count the cost. This is the only way even to approach experiential religion in the modern church.

Here is another reason for the church to have a period of waiting after a person makes a profession of faith before he is received into full membership. Since we are human and do not have divine insight, this waiting period can give the church a chance to evaluate the convert's understanding of his mission and his commitment to the lordship of Christ. In all this the church would be seeking to recapture and maintain the real vitality of the New Testament faith.

Salvation—Point and Process

Is salvation a position or a relationship? Is it a mechanical transaction or a dynamic process? Is it a static possession or a moving spiritual reality that continues to grow? In our practice we seem to have magnified the former alternatives and in so doing we have tended to interpret salvation in too narrow and too superficial a fashion. To some the grace of God is dispensed simply because a man has cried, "Lord, Lord!" Forgiveness becomes a "cosmic blotter" that "gets one off" from his sins. Salvation is a "free pass" into heaven, unrelated to the quality of one's life. Have one experience, make a certain profession, go through certain forms, and the whole issue of external destiny is decided and sealed. Once the individual is "saved" he can do what he pleases and have nothing to worry about.

There is not one shred of biblical support for such a position. In the New Testament we find no justification for such a cheap and easy interpretation of salvation. It is a tradition of man parading as the doctrine of God. Rather, the statement of Jesus was, "Not every one that saith unto me, Lord, Lord, shall enter into the kingdom of heaven; but he that doeth the will of my Father which is in heaven" (Matt. 7:21).

Although the initial experience with Christ does not constitute the whole of the saving relationship, salvation does have a beginning. Forces and factors leading up to conversion may begin in earliest infancy and continue through childhood. Sometimes the whole process is so gradual that when the individual makes his public profession of faith, he cannot point to a time or place and say this is when God worked his miracle of grace—regeneration. With another (usually with one who is older or who has lived more deeply in sin) the experience of regeneration may be cataclysmic in nature and thus datable. But in both instances there is a beginning—a conscious entering into a relationship and union with Christ through faith.

This emphasis on the initial experience as the basis for salvation is needed to counteract the view that one may "grow naturally" into the kingdom of God on the basis of ethical achievement. It can also counteract the idea that a child may grow up in a Christian home and in the church, take a course in premembership training, and be received automatically into the church.[19] The individual may never have entered into any valid or saving relationship with Christ at all. Salvation comes only on the basis of a conscious, decisive encounter with Christ. Raines insists on the necessity for "a conversion in which there is a beginning but no ending; a conversion in which there are both crisis and process, in which one is constantly by grace through faith becoming a Christian." [20] In such a decisive encounter, in crisis or in calm, God works his miracle of regeneration. Later encounters may be more emotional or they may be deeper, but this one is unique as a spiritual "watershed," the turning point in personal experience.

A distinction needs to be made between regeneration and conversion. It is unfortunate that in popular usage the two are synonymous. Actually, conversion is a "turning from something to something" and thus the individual may be "converted" many times in his life. For example, Jesus said to Peter, "When thou art converted, strengthen thy brethren" (Luke 22:32). But he was regenerated only once.

Salvation does have a beginning, but we have so magnified the beginning experience that we have almost completely lost sight of the fact that salvation is also process. In the New Testament, salvation is spoken of as past event, continuing ex-

---

[19] The practice of insisting on a conscious "decision for Christ" may also become mechanical and meaningless as indicated in this chapter and the next.

[20] Robert A. Raines, *New Life in the Church* (New York: Harper & Bros., 1961), p. 22.

perience, and future expectation.[21] For example, in Ephesians
2:8 it is spoken of as a completed and continuing fact, "By
grace have ye been saved." The verb tense is a perfect para-
phrastic, indicating a completed action that is still going on.
Some react against this view of salvation as a completed act or
accomplished fact, perhaps because of the way it is abused.
Others see it as the whole of salvation. Both extremes are,
erroneous. While a valid part of the New Testament concept
of salvation, it is only a part, not the whole. (See also Rom.
8:24; 2 Tim. 1:9; and Titus 3:5).

In 1 Corinthians 1:18 the emphasis is on the process of
salvation in referring "to us who are being saved." The tense
here is present participle denoting continuing action. Throughout life we live in the state of being saved. This helps us to
understand properly the dynamic nature of the salvation relationship. (See also Acts 2:47, 1 Cor. 15:2; 2 Cor. 2:15.)

Finally, there is the emphasis on the culmination of the
process. The complete fruition of salvation is a future hope
toward which we joyfully and confidently look. "We shall be
saved from wrath through him" (Rom. 5:9). God has provided "an inheritance . . . reserved in heaven for you . . . unto
salvation ready to be revealed in the last time" (1 Peter 1:4-5).
(See also Matt. 10:22; Rom. 13:11; Phil. 2:12; Heb. 9:28.) The
salvation which we experience now is an "earnest" of the inheritance which is laid up for us (2 Cor. 1:22; 5:5; Eph. 1:14).

Can a Person Have a "Saved Soul" but a "Lost Life"?

One question has arisen in the background of our consideration of the nature of authentic faith that now must be faced
directly: Is it possible for a person to have a "saved soul" but
a "lost life"?[22] In our desire to magnify the fact that man's
works contribute nothing to his salvation but that salvation is
wholly by grace through faith, we have tended to answer this

---

[21] G. Abbott-Smith, A Manual Greek Lexicon of the New Testament (3rd
ed.; Edinburgh: T. & T. Clark, 1937), p. 436.

[22] Cf. "Is Growth in the Christian Life Optional?" discussed in chapter 5.

question in the affirmative. Our evangelistic approach has been strongly influenced by this affirmative answer. But is it really true?

Before going on, the question must be carefully defined. What is meant by "lost life"? If it means that the individual may be converted on his "death bed" and thus all his past life is lost so far as its counting for Christ is concerned, then the answer to our question would be "yes." Or if "lost life" means that the basic pattern of the individual's life is "in Christ" but due to neglect or for some other reason he fails to fulfil his maximum potential as a Christian, the answer would still be "yes," for this would include all of us. On the other hand, if "lost life" means that, although the individual has made a "decision for Christ," the pattern of his life is not "in Christ" so that he gives no evidence that he either has understood or has committed himself to the purpose for which God called him as a Christian, the answer is "no." It is this last meaning with which we are concerned in this discussion.

The very phrasing of the question (presenting "soul" and "life" as though they were separate entities) indicates the extent to which our modern religious thought patterns have been influenced by Greek philosophy rather than by biblical teachings. Greek philosophy viewed man as a duality, soul and body. Man had a spiritual essence which resided in a physical or material body. In this view it was possible to deal with one of the aspects of man without necessarily dealing with the other. Thus, from the perspective of the Greek it would be possible for a person to have a "saved soul" but a "lost life."

There is nothing in Scripture, however, to support this view of man; it is utterly foreign to Hebrew thought. In the teachings of Scripture, man is a unity. As White indicates,

Greek thought distinguished sharply between body and soul, and some held the body to be essentially evil and temporary, while the soul sought to escape from it into the realm of spirit. . . . To the Hebrew mind, on the other hand, . . . human personality was regarded as a unity, an animated body, and the soul was the divine life inbreathed into the body and inseparable from it.[23]

To understand the biblical view, as opposed to Greek philosophy, it is necessary to consider the meaning of such words as "soul," "spirit," "body," and "life." In Hebrew thought "soul" was "the breath of life," "one's essential being," "the totality of his existence." One's soul or life could not be separated from his essential existence. When *psyche* (soul) is in any way differentiated from *pneuma* (spirit), it refers to "the natural life of earthly man. . . . Man does not consist of two parts, much less of three. . . . Rather, man is a living unity." [24]

Man as a whole person is often referred to in Scripture by the word *soma* or "body." In many instances one could simply substitute the appropriate personal pronoun in place of "body," for instance: "Christ shall be magnified in my body" [me] (Phil. 1:20). "I beseech you therefore, brethren, by the mercies of God, that ye present your bodies [selves] a living sacrifice" (Rom. 12:1). "This is my body [self] which is given for you" (Luke 22:19). The soul-body unity was so deep in Hebrew thought that the Bible places the emphasis on the resurrection of the body rather than on the "immortality of the soul," which is a Greek concept.[25] "There is no *anima immortalis*, but only a personality, destined by God for eternity, a person who is body-soul-spirit, who dies as a whole, and is raised as a whole." [26]

It is utterly fallacious to say that a person can have a saved soul and a lost life, implying that the "soul" or the essential self may be saved while his "life," that which is expressed in and through the body, is lost. This is to imply that the body has a mind and will, separate from one's essential self, which controls its actions or life. This is completely false. It is man in his essential being that controls and directs his body, his

---

[23] *Op. cit.*, p. 109.

[24] Rudolf Bultmann, *Theology of the New Testament* (New York: Charles Scribner's Sons, 1951), I, 205, 209.

[25] Cf. Oscar Cullmann, *Immortality of the Soul or Resurrection of the Dead? The Witness of the New Testament* (London: The Epworth Press, 1958).

[26] Brunner, *op. cit.*, p. 363, n.

acts, his life. The body cannot act apart from the essential being of man. Man's life (activity of the body) is merely the expression of the *psyche* (soul) or man's essential self, for this is the source of those actions or that life. Soul and flesh were sometimes distinguished in Hebrew usage, but they were not thought of as two fundamentally different forms of existence. "Heart, glory, soul, and flesh all mean the whole man in different manifestations." [27]

In the Bible one's life is always associated with his "walk" (or pattern of life) and is usually followed by a qualifying adverb or descriptive phrase. "Walk worthy of God" (1 Thess. 2:12). "Let us walk honestly" (Rom. 13:13). "For we are his workmanship, created in Christ Jesus unto good works, which God hath before ordained that we should walk in them" (Eph. 2:10). "Be bold against some, which think of us as if we walked according to the flesh" (2 Cor. 10:2). Life is lived in some sphere and it is this sphere that gives life its direction, i.e., "in Christ" or "in the world." Thus, we come to see that

"salvation" and "sanctification" are not the completely separate and distinct aspects of spiritual life that theologians and expositors, with their love for "headings," seem to imply. Paul wrote the letter to the Romans very largely to dispel such an idea, and to insist that no man can claim to be saved by faith and still continue in sin. For *by that faith which saves him* he has already taken his place with Christ upon the cross, and died to sin—the crucial point of his sanctification is already achieved in the repentant trust which makes him Christ's.[28]

James D. Smart calls attention to the tendency on the part of the modern church to separate salvation from life.

What is happening to men in the social, economic, and political spheres is regarded as a secular matter to be left to the social scientists, economists, and politicians and not to be touched by the minister. Any one of the prophets, and Jesus with them, would have

---

[27] Kenneth Grayston in *A Theological Word Book of the Bible,* ed. Alan Richardson (New York: The Macmillan Co., 1950), p. 83.
[28] White, *op. cit.,* p. 204.

been aghast at such a conception of man. Biblically the soul is defined as the total self of man. He does not have a soul; he *is* a soul. Inner and outer life are inseparable.[29]

The evangelistic approach that holds it is possible to have a "saved soul" but a "lost life" is not only erroneous; it is dangerous. According to Farmer this "egocentric desire for an enjoyable state of mind," this desire to have one's soul saved, this "flight from the divine 'Thou' in His immediate absolute claim upon the will here and now," is "undoubtedly the most universal perversion and distortion of true religion that there is." [30] The extreme to which such an erroneous view leads is seen in a conversation reliably reported between a Sunday school teacher in a Baptist church and a member of a Junior class. The class was discussing the matter of salvation. One boy asked the teacher, "Was Hitler a Christian?" The teacher replied, "He certainly didn't act like one. We can only hope he trusted Jesus when he was a little boy!" Admittedly this may be an extreme incident, but it illustrates a viewpoint which is altogether too prevalent.

Conversion in either its biblical or etymological meaning does not refer simply to a highly emotional or mystical experience in which a person's "soul" is saved. Rather it refers to a change in the manner of one's life. Etymologically it is a "turning from" and a "turning to." "For they themselves shew of us what manner of entering in we had unto you, and how ye turned to God from idols to serve the living and true God" (1 Thess. 1:9).

In our evangelistic approach we have magnified properly the fact that salvation was wholly by grace and by God's act alone. Our problem, however, has been that we have failed to emphasize adequately the nature of man's response to God. God accomplishes his work of grace in the human life only on the basis of a relational response. Authentic faith for Paul did not consist simply of a mystical, emotional experience, nor was

[20] *The Rebirth of Ministry,* p. 57.
[30] *Op. cit.,* p. 150.

it merely intellectual belief in certain ideas. "We die 'with Christ' and 'rise with Christ to newness of life.' This was Paul's answer to the charge that his Gospel of salvation by faith alone allows a man to continue in sin." [31]

The pattern of one's life does not save him, but the pattern of one's life does indicate the quality of the relationship or union into which he has entered with God. The church that is primarily concerned with saving a man's "soul" apart from his "life" (man in his essential relationships) is following a nonbiblical approach to evangelism. This approach forsakes the Bible and follows Greek philosophy. According to the biblical view man cannot have a "saved soul" and a "lost life." Thus, in our approach to evangelism we must emphasize the fact that when man is saved, he is saved in the totality of his being, and this inevitably means his life in the here and now. Bonhoeffer puts the matter clearly:

The only man who has the right to say that he is justified by grace alone is the man who has left all to follow Christ. Such a man knows that the call to discipleship is a gift of grace, and that the call is inseparable from the grace. But those who try to use this grace as a dispensation from following Christ are simply deceiving themselves.[32]

---

[31] White, *op. cit.*, p. 45.
[32] *Op. cit.*, p. 43.

Part IV

Seeking a Regenerate Church Membership

10

Do We Have a Regenerate
Church Membership?

A regenerate church membership has been for Baptists a cardinal doctrine. In *The Axioms of Religion*, Mullins stated that "the ecclesiastical significance of the Baptists is a regenerated church-membership." [1] As second in a series of seven essential principles which have been held as fundamental in Baptist thought and life, Augustus H. Strong listed "credible evidence of regeneration and conversion as prerequisite to church-membership." [2] W. T. Conner, long-time seminary professor, wrote: "That the church should be composed of the regenerate only, the New Testament makes clear. . . . Moreover, the nature and mission of the church carries with it the view that only regenerate people should belong to the church." [3]

Historically the Somerset (Particular Baptist) Confession (1656) states,

That in admitting of members into the church of Christ, it is the duty of the church, and ministers whom it concerns, in faithfulness to God, that they be careful they receive none but such as do make forth evident demonstration of the new birth, and the work of faith with power. [4]

In addition

both the Philadelphia (1743, 1798) and Charleston (1774) Baptist

[1] E. Y. Mullins, *The Axioms of Religion* (Philadelphia: The Judson Press, 1908), pp. 56-57.

[2] *Systematic Theology* (New York: Press of E. R. Andrews, 1886), p. 495.

[3] *Christian Doctrine* (Nashville: Broadman Press, 1937), p. 260.

[4] William L. Lumpkin, *Baptist Confessions of Faith* (Philadelphia: The Judson Press, 1959), p. 211.

Church Disciplines prescribe procedures for the admission of members in the light of the concept of "visible saints" and "regenerate members." "None are fit materials for a Gospel-Church," said the Charleston Church Discipline, "without having first experienced an entire change of nature." To open the door of admission "so wide as to suffer unbelievers, unconverted and graceless persons to crowd into it without control" is "to make the Church of Christ a harlot."[5]

Infant Baptism Rejected

Churches of the free church tradition contend that this is another area where the Reformation was stopped short.[6] The reformed churches by "retaining the practice of paedobaptism and the union of church and state, . . . continued an ecclesiastical system which inadvertently perpetuated the evils of an unregenerate church membership."[7] Anabaptists withstood both Luther and Zwingli on this point at the risk of their lives. It is at this point that the Anabaptists disclaimed that they were a part of the movement to *reform* the church. Rather it was their contention that they were seeking to *restore* the church to its original New Testament pattern. In its essence the doctrine of a regenerate church membership means that a local congregation is to be composed of only those who have given and continue to give evidence that they have been regenerated by the grace and work of God and thus have become new creatures in Christ. On the basis of this doctrine, Baptists have been emphatic in their insistence upon "believer's baptism" and in their rejection of infant baptism.

Those who practice infant baptism generally hold that this rite has both instrumental and symbolic significance. "The Ministration of Holy Baptism" given in *The Book of Common Prayer* states "that *this Child* is regenerate, and grafted into the body of Christ's Church." [8] Ruel Howe says: "In Baptism

---

[5] James Leo Garrett, "Seeking a Regenerate Church Membership," *Southwestern Journal of Theology*, III, April, 1961, p. 29.

[6] *Supra*, pp. 100f.

[7] Robert G. Torbet, *A History of the Baptists* (Philadelphia: The Judson Press, 1950), p. 476.

[8] Milwaukee: Morehouse Publishing Co., 1929, p. 280.

God acts instrumentally at the time of the rite while we are standing around the font. The relationship of this child to God as His child is declared and sealed so that he is received as 'a member of Christ, a Child of God, and inheritor of the Kingdom of Heaven.' " [9] The practice of infant baptism is generally based on a sacramental view of the church or on a covenant theology.

To be properly understood, however, baptism must be placed in the context of the incarnation, the cross, and the resurrection of Jesus. That is, baptism, theologically speaking, must be viewed within the framework of the total redemptive work of God in Christ. Salvation cannot "be effected outside of, apart from, over the head of man. To deny this would be to deny both the principle of incarnation and the pattern of the life and death of the incarnate Son." [10]

The practice of infant baptism is rejected not only because it lacks a basis in Scripture but also because its practice violates a basic biblical principle, namely, the necessity for conscious and personal choice in salvation. Those who have sought to justify this practice on the basis of Jesus' statements concerning children and the baptizing of "households" have failed in their efforts.[11] Karl Barth caused consternation and stimulated vigorous discussion among reformed theologians with his monograph rejecting infant baptism, particularly with reference to its instrumental value.

One cannot properly maintain . . . that water-baptism conferred by the Church is *as such* a causative or generative means by which there are imparted to man the forgiveness of sins, the Holy Spirit and even faith. . . . From the New Testament standpoint it is impossible to say that "everyone who is born of Christian parents is born into the Christian Church *(Gemeinde)*." . . . From the stand-

---

[9] *Man's Need and God's Action* (Greenwich, Conn.: Seabury Press, 1953), p. 54.

[10] Neville Clark, "The Theology of Baptism" in Gilmore, *Christian Baptism, op. cit.*, p. 313.

[11] R. E. O. White, *The Biblical Doctrine of Initiation* (Grand Rapids: Wm. B. Eerdmans Publishing Co., 1960), pp. 329-338.

point of a doctrine of baptism, infant-baptism can hardly be preserved without exegetical and practical artifices and sophisms—the
proof to the contrary has yet to be supplied![12]

He suggested that perhaps the main reason the reformers held
to the practice of infant baptism was that they did not want
to renounce the concept of a national church. They were
afraid that if they were to break with the practice of infant
baptism and insist on believer's baptism, "the Church would
not easily any longer be a people's church in the sense of a
state Church or a church of the masses." [13] He states that on
one occasion Luther confessed that not many would be baptized if they had to rely on believer's baptism. Thus, an unconscious desire for "numbers" may underlie the practice of
infant baptism.

Although he held a covenant theology and defended the
practice of infant baptism, Horace Bushnell, often called the
father of modern religious education, vigorously rejected the
view that infant baptism had any instrumental significance.
If in the baptismal service it is said that the child has his sins
remitted, this has no meaning because the infant has no sins
which need remitting. If it is said that the corrupted nature
of the child is transformed, the child, in due time, will demonstrate that this is not so. "And thus it turns out . . . that the
grace magnified in the beginning, by words of so high an
import, is a thing of no value—it is nothing. . . . There is not
enough of import in it to save the meaning of the rite." [14]

When the instrumental value of infant baptism is rejected,
however, the rite tends to lose its symbolic significance. Those
who insist that infant baptism is analogous to circumcision
among the Jews need to be reminded that even for the Jews
this rite was not ultimately decisive. Paul pointed out: "For he
is not a Jew, which is one outwardly; neither is that circum-

[12] *Op. cit.*, pp. 26, 44, 49. Cullmann countered Barth's views with an able,
though not convincing, rebuttal.

[13] *Ibid.*, pp. 52-53.

[14] *Christian Nurture* (New York: Charles Scribner's Sons, 1916), p. 95.

cision, which is outward in the flesh: but he is a Jew, which is one inwardly; and circumcision is that of the heart, in the spirit, and not in the letter" (Rom. 2:28-29).

In the final analysis that which is decisive for the child is not the symbolic significance of the rite but the *quality* of the fellowship with which the child is surrounded, and the response he comes to make to God through this fellowship. Those practicing this rite hold that the child is thus brought into the fellowship of the church and is accepted as, and is made to feel that he is, a part of the body of Christ. Again, however, in spite of words of high-sounding intent, the child does not become completely a part of that fellowship. For example, he is not allowed to partake of the Lord's Supper. The child recognizes that he is not fully a part of that fellowship at this stage of his life. He recognizes that there is another rite through which he must go at a later period of his life.

Some feel that the churches which do not practice infant baptism have actually surrounded their young children with more of a sense of loving concern, more genuine fellowship, more of the "aids to grace," than has been true in some churches which practice the rite. Those who practice infant baptism, particularly those who emphasize its symbolic significance, insist that its primary value is in calling the attention of the church and parents to their responsibility and obligation in providing for the child the proper kind of Christian nurture. In practice, however, it often has had the opposite effect.

This points up a serious danger in the practice of infant baptism and suggests still another reason it is rejected. What Bushnell referred to as being "potentially regenerate" tends too often—in the mind of the child, parent, and church—to slip over into the area of being "actually regenerate." Bushnell somewhat heatedly denounced the idea that through this rite the child becomes actually regenerate. When interpreted with this instrumental emphasis, "the rite," he said, "is fertile only in maintaining a superstition. . . . By a motion of his hand the priest breaks in, to interrupt and displace all the laws of character in life. . . . A superstitious homage collects about his person. The child looks on him as one who opens heaven by a ceremony! The ungodly parent hurries to him, to get the regenerative grace for his dying child." [15] Yet with those who view the rite only symbolically, this same attitude sometimes develops. Parents insist on having their child baptized. They, then, feel that the "big job" is done. The church receives him into "the body of Christ," and the distinction between being "potentially regenerate" and "actually regenerate" is sometimes lost.

When this happens, the church has failed to emphasize those elements of genuine encounter, personal choice, and depth of commitment which are essential to the new life in Christ. When one understands what the New Testament means by authentic faith and becomes aware of the radical demands of the Christian life in terms of mission and ministry, it is apparent that this confrontation and depth of commitment are truly fundamental in a saving relationship. This happens only on the basis of personal choice.

The churches that practice infant baptism provide the opportunity for such choice at the time of confirmation. In addition, these churches follow the excellent plan of providing confirmation classes (or premembership classes) for the children prior to their acceptance as members. These classes last from three months to a year or longer. A person's decision for Christ ought to be an intelligent decision, but simply to give religious instruction before confirmation does not necessarily nor automatically lead to experiential religion. The candidates may have knowledge about Christ but lack the relational experience with Christ which alone leads to salvation. Randolph C. Miller points to the practice in England and West Germany as evidence of this fact. There the children receive religious instruction under the best qualified teachers using the finest curriculum. Worship is also a part of this experience. It is quite probable that the youth of these countries have a greater

---

[15] *Ibid.,* pp. 95, 96.

knowledge of the Christian faith than young Christians in any other country. The difficulty is that there is

practically no transfer to Church loyalty. In West Germany, according to information from Church youth leaders, the children are confirmed at fourteen years of age, and this is the occasion for social celebrations. Most of them leave school at the same age and usually begin work. But only a minority of them are found in Church-sponsored meetings or at worship. Somewhere along the way, in spite of lengthy confirmation instruction from their pastors their intellectual grasp of Biblical information has failed to make any connection with the Christian community.[16]

Miller says that in this country confirmation often becomes a form of "graduation." The adolescent has become an "adult" and is no longer expected to attend the church school. In fact, in some cases the candidate may have "decided for confirmation or its equivalent because this will take the pressure off and he can do as he pleases; and this does not include going to Church." [17]

But those churches that insist on individual choice and believer's baptism also have problems that need to be brought into focus. First, although these churches insist on a free, personal choice, that choice may be based on nothing deeper than a desire of a child to please a Sunday school teacher or to follow the example of a playmate who joined the church the month before. The subtle pressure put on children by well-meaning but misguided Sunday school teachers or department superintendents who pride themselves on the fact that no child has ever gone out of their class (or department) without being "saved" has led to many mechanical and superficial decisions.

The second problem these churches need to face is the seeming trend toward baptizing children at an increasingly younger age. Three generations ago the majority made their decision in their early teens. The last two generations found this age of decision-making lowered to the junior years (9-12

---

[16] Miller, *op. cit.*, p. 2.
[17] *Ibid.*, p. 46.

years). In this generation there is an increasing number of primary age children (6-8) making "decisions for Christ." Recently in a large Southern Baptist church a four-year-old child was baptized and received into full membership. We reject infant baptism, but if the present trend continues, we will be practicing it in another generation or two.

We reject infant baptism because we insist that a person must make a responsible and conscious decision for Christ. If the Christian life is a mission to which a person gives himself, if he must understand the nature of this mission in order to make an intelligent response to it, how young is "too young" for a child, in view of his limited maturity, to make a truly responsible decision for Christ? Many of these children follow through with their commitment for the rest of life. But the question must also be raised, What about the large number who do not "follow through"? What is their condition?

The point being made is: In salvation is it the quality of relationship and the depth of commitment that are ultimately decisive, or is it the particular mode of receiving the individual for church membership? The experiential philosophy insists that salvation comes only in encounter with Christ. It does not come by proxy. Knowledge is involved, but it does not necessarily come through information gained in an instruction class. It is based on personal decision, but is not necessarily involved in a profession of faith. The external approach which the church sets up, while important, is secondary. It is the quality of relationship that is central.

An Analysis of the Present Situation

The basic thesis of Part IV, however, is that the doctrine of a regenerate church membership which has been held so long and professed so proudly by Baptists has been woefully misunderstood and inadequately practiced in the life of the modern churches. The rejection of infant baptism is only one aspect of this doctrine. Two important emphases have been seriously neglected. First, the doctrine of a regenerate church membership places upon the church the obligation to utilize every means possible to insure that those who are admitted to membership, whatever their age, are truly regenerate. This positive emphasis is just as binding upon the church as is the negative emphasis on rejecting infant baptism. Second, this doctrine means that the church must practice the New Testament view of discipline to insure that growth and purity will be maintained in the life of the membership. The loss of these two emphases has been a significant contributing factor in the growing institutionalism and the consequent loss of spiritual power in the life of the modern church. These two emphases must be reclaimed by the church if we are to recapture experiential religion.

In this area, one cannot be dogmatic. There is no objective criterion by which one may determine with finality whether another is regenerate. In addition, even the one who is a "new creature" remains a sinner and in his life will fall far short of the "glory of God." With our finite minds how are we to distinguish between regenerate sinners and the unregenerate sinners? However complex the problem, the church with all its finite limitations is still under binding obligation to seek to approach the ideal. Either we ought to seek seriously to implement this doctrine in practice or else repudiate it.

Some will contend that we are already following this doctrine in our practice. Their position is that this doctrine simply teaches that the church should reject infant baptism. Thus, it is now necessary to inquire how effective has been the current emphasis simply on the rejection of infant baptism in approaching the ideal of a regenerate church membership.

Having no objective criterion as the basis of evaluation and lacking divine insight, we can seek an answer to this question only in general terms. Speaking of Protestantism in general, one writer estimates that "about half of all persons who join churches drop by the wayside in the first six months." [18] E. Stanley Jones divides church members into three groups. First,

---

[18] Cox, *op. cit.*, p. 27.

there are those to whom religion is "firsthand, vital, and life changing." Second, there are those with whom religion is only a secondhand experience. Primarily their faith comes not from God but from their surroundings, "from books, from services, from relatives, from social custom." When they are transplanted from this environment to some other environment less conducive to religion, they do not have sufficient faith to withstand the strain of this transplantation. Thus, when they move, they drop out of the church. Then there is the third group which has neither a firsthand nor a secondhand religion. They are just externally related to the church. "So within the church only about one third of the people know what conversion is in any vital way. The other two thirds need conversion." [19]

Another writer claims that in connection with a recent evangelistic campaign those who were preparing for it "were praying that 50 per cent of the converts might stand. In anticipation of the campaign they had judged that a fifty-fifty result would be satisfactory." [20] This is both a tragedy and a travesty. No pastor, no evangelist, no church has the right to traffic thus in the souls of men!

It is true that difficulties and dangers are involved in any serious effort to seek the ideal of a regenerate church membership, but it should also be remembered that the church stands under the judgment of God for those lax practices that lead to an unregenerate church membership. Thus the choice is not simply between an easy way and a dangerous and difficult way. The choice is between a right way and a wrong way, between what is God's way and what is not. The church stands under judgment for her decision in this matter. Thus, she must be willing to search and seriously seek to find and follow God's way, regardless of whether it happens to be easy or dangerous and difficult.

---

[19] *Op. cit.*, pp. 9, 10.
[20] Owen Brandon, *The Battle for the Soul* (Philadelphia: The Westminster Press, 1960), p. 70.

Now let us explore this matter as it relates to Southern Baptists specifically. In 1945 they undertook the worthy objective of seeking to win a million people to Christ in one year. G. S. Dobbins, recognizing the danger involved, wrote, "As matters now stand, if Southern Baptists should add one million new church members to their rolls, they would at the same time add approximately six hundred thousand to the number of the unenlisted!" [21] That is, the approach to evangelism practiced by Baptists would anticipate the loss of six out of every ten that were "won." Dobbins did not mean to imply that all of these six would be unregenerate. But neither is it to be inferred that all would be regenerate simply because they made a profession or because they had an emotional experience. It is interesting to note that his estimate is strikingly similar to the one given by E. Stanley Jones.

Another survey conducted recently among Southern Baptists indicated that "for each ten members who join our churches for baptism, ten years later, two of them have died, one has dropped out, three have become non-resident, while four are still resident members of some local church. In addition, not more than 50 per cent of those who are resident members are really active in the life of the church." [22] Thus a conservative estimate would be that at least 50 per cent of our total membership is inactive, that is, they are either nonresident or almost totally unenlisted.

Approximately one out of every three members of Southern Baptist churches are classified as nonresident. In 1960 there were 2,670,047 reported. This was an increase of 121,055 in one year. This increase in nonresident members nearly matched the increase in resident membership of 125,260 for the same year! Less than 50 per cent of our total membership is enrolled in Sunday school. Added to this, on any given Sunday only

---

[21] "Achieving a Great Goal and Avoiding a Grave Danger," *The Review and Expositor*, October, 1944, p. 410.

[22] Luther Joe Thompson, "Checked Your 'Back Door' Lately?" *The Baptist Program*, August, 1959, p. 9.

slightly over 50 per cent of those enrolled are in attendance at Sunday school. There are exceptions, but the general rule holds that the large majority of those who are not enrolled in Bible study are not related to any other part of the organized life of the church. Less than 25 per cent of the total membership is enrolled in Training Union and only 55 per cent of these are present on any given Sunday.[23]

These statistics are not given to imply that a regenerate church membership is to be determined by one's relationship with the Sunday school, with the church membership training program, or with any other aspect of the organized life of the church. Varied circumstances and contributing factors both in the individual's life and in the life of the church may account for a practical level of enlistment. This is simply one way of getting some objective data concerning one aspect of the life of the church. The essential nature of this life includes a call to a mission—to share in God's redemptive purpose in the world. This mission is fulfilled through a ministry in the world. The life "in Christ" is a growing life. Salvation is not a position; it is a dynamic relationship. Growth in this life is not optional with the individual.

If all this is true, then one indication that a person is "in Christ" is that he is growing in his ability to enter into and fulfil the mission for which he was called. If the individual gives no evidence that he is growing but rather persistently rejects all opportunities afforded him for such growth, then a serious question may be raised as to whether the individual truly is "in Christ." When we add to this the facts that the spiritual life in our churches is low, the effectiveness of our witness to the world is weak, and our power against evil is ineffective, the seriousness of the situation becomes even more apparent.

How did these people who demonstrate no real understanding of the meaning of the Christian faith and who demon-

---

[23] Cf. Porter Routh, "Personally," *The Baptist Program*, March, 1962, pp. 8. 30.

strate no genuine commitment to the purposes of Christ get into our Baptist churches? We cannot blame infant baptism because we do not follow this practice. The evidence seems to indicate that those who practice infant baptism are about as successful in having a regenerate church membership as those who reject infant baptism. If this is correct, then the conclusion is inescapable that the rejection of infant baptism alone is not a sufficient foundation upon which to build a regenerate church membership.

Contributing Causes

Numerous factors undoubtedly have contributed to our present condition. Two of them have been discussed in previous chapters. In the first place, the image that the church has presented to the world as to what it means to be a Christian has been weak and limited. That is, when we invited people to accept Christ, we were inviting them (so they seemed to understand) to something that was different from the mission and ministry to which God was calling. We were inviting them to something that was less than *the* way of the New Testament. Unfortunately, the life lived by the church did not demonstrate the true nature of this life as mission and ministry. Thus the potential candidate had no way of knowing that his inadequate view was erroneous.

In the second place, our approach to evangelism has been defective. We have failed to lead potential converts to understand adequately what is involved in a genuine saving relationship with God. The particular period in the cycle toward institutionalism in which we find ourselves as a denomination undoubtedly has contributed to this approach in evangelism. We have reached the stage of remarkable success. We have experienced rapid growth in every area of denominational life. Thus, we feel impelled to continue to grow in order to continue to be successful. This growth has been interpreted as an evidence of God's favor upon us. Any decline in growth would be interpreted as a withdrawal of God's favor.

In addition, our denomination has a large and complex program at home and around the world that must be financed. Thus any decrease in evangelism, in enrolments in the organizations, and in the budgets would be cause for serious alarm. To show such alarm is only natural. There is no particular merit in decreases in the life of the church (unless this is necessary for the church to recapture her mission and vitality). The point is, however, when a denomination has been highly successful, it feels that it must continue to expand.

As Smart contends, too often

this emphasis upon growth leads easily to a lowering of standards, so that people are swept into the membership of the church without any adequate preparation for it, without any clear confrontation with the claims of the gospel and so without any real decision of faith. The apology for this procedure is sometimes made that now at least they are within the circle of the church and the church has the opportunity of reaching them with its gospel. But when they find so many already inside the church who know little more of what it all means than they do, are they likely to take seriously their need for anything more? [24]

Thus, defective evangelism contributes to an unregenerate church membership.

Two additional factors that have contributed to our present situation need now to be considered, namely, the inadequacy of our present mode of receiving new members and our failure to practice the New Testament view of Christian discipline in both its formative and reformative aspects.

---

[24] *Op. cit.*, pp. 152.

11

A Period of Waiting and
a Regenerate Church Membership

Without seeking to separate causes from symptoms, James Leo Garrett lists five factors related to the problem of admission to church membership that have contributed to the current condition. First, there is the failure to have any serious or vocal confession of one's faith when the candidate applies for membership. Instead, there is the practice of the pastor's confessing faith for the applicant to the congregation—"a strange proxy method for Baptists!" Second, there is a lack of any serious doctrinal or ethical standards as prerequisite for membership. A third factor is the "subtle pressures toward quantitative or numerical gains in church membership." Too often success is measured by the number of additions reported. From many sources the pressure is on the pastor "to produce results!" Fourth, there is the use of questionable methods to provoke premature professions of faith by young children. Fifth, "there is the widespread practice of taking the congregational vote on new members immediately after the applicant presents himself for membership." [1]

The present practice of receiving candidates into the membership of the church immediately upon their profession of faith is not conducive to a regenerate church membership. The proposal being made here is that the church ought to have a period of waiting [2] between the individual's profession of faith and the time he is received into full church membership.

---

[1] *Op. cit.*, pp. 31-32.

[2] Because it sounds so passive, this is not an accurate term. Some phrase denoting the opportunity of the period for study, growth, and demonstration would be more appropriate.

A. H. Strong suggests that it is the responsibility of the church to "require of all candidates for baptism credible evidence of regeneration." This

duty of the church to gain credible evidence of regeneration in the case of every person admitted to the body involves its right to require of candidates, in addition to a profession of faith with the lips, some satisfactory proof that this profession is accompanied by change in the conduct.[3]

If "credible evidence" is required before a person is received into membership, time is required. In no other way can this "satisfactory proof'" be supplied! In fairness, it should be stated that Strong did not favor a period of waiting. Thus, he reveals an inconsistency in his position. How is it possible for one to give "credible evidence" of any serious nature without a lapse of time being involved? As the reformers failed to carry certain basic Reformation principles to their logical conclusion, Baptists have failed to carry the basic implications of a regenerate church membership to its logical conclusion and insist on a period of waiting before receiving members into the church.

To implement the practice of a period of waiting, it is further proposed that the church should have two types of membership. "Professing members" would be those who had been received on the basis of their "profession of faith." "Full members" would have demonstrated by "credible evidence" the reality of their profession. Robert W. Spike seems to concur with this suggestion:

Some modern adaptation of the relationship between catechumens and the baptized in the early church must emerge. . . . One of the most obvious implications of such a concept is that full membership in the church should not be possible without sufficient experience in the life, worship, and study of the church, so that its full significance is clear.[4]

---

[3] *Op. cit.*, p. 533.
[4] *Op. cit.*, pp. 18-19.

It must be clearly understood that this suggested period of waiting has absolutely nothing to do with a person's salvation. That is, if a person has had an encounter with Christ in which he has entered into a genuine, saving relationship, he is saved. Having a waiting period for him will not make him any less saved. He will be surrounded by all the fellowship of the church while he is a professing member. The converse of this also needs to be noted. If the individual has not entered into a real saving relationship with Christ, immediate full membership will not save him.

Of course no individual or group can determine with inerrant finality whether or not a person is saved. God alone knows this. The church has the right and the responsibility, however, to determine whether an individual will go out *with the sanction of the church* as a representative of Jesus Christ.

Reasons for a Period of Waiting

There are several reasons why this period of waiting is desperately needed in the life of the modern churches. First, it is needed so that the church itself will come to understand more clearly that growth is essential for the one who has just made a profession of faith. The church has paid lip service to the idea of Christian growth. A waiting period will serve as a prolonged reminder to the church that it must express an intensive and continuing concern for the individual after he has made his initial decision. Instead of the present practice expressing *primary* concern in seeking the individual's initial decision for Christ and then simply *hoping* that he will take advantage of the church-provided opportunities for growth, the church will insist that the individual is *expected* to grow. If anything the church may express even greater concern for the individual *after* he has made his initial decision, and it will provide intensive and specialized opportunities for study and experiences leading to growth.[5]

If for any reason the individual fails to take advantage of

---

[5] The outline of this course of study is given on page 230.

these opportunities or seems to be distinterested in growth, the church will intensify its expressions of concern for him. It will indicate to the individual that the "in Christ" relationship is a growing relationship. It will express concerned warnings as to what his refusal to grow *might* imply as to his relationship with God. The church must recognize the period immediately following the individual's initial decision almost as a crisis period. In its expression of concern and in its program the church must treat this period of the person's development with the utmost care.

In the second place, this period of waiting is needed so that the individual who makes a profession of faith will understand that growth in the Christian life is essential. The church must not be deceptive at this point. Both church and convert must understand more clearly the radical nature of the call of God to discipleship. Let us assume that the church in ministering to a given individual has led him to make a profession of faith in Christ as Lord and Saviour. The church must say to the individual (which also should have been made clear to him before he made his profession), "You have said that you have united your life with God in Christ. That is wonderful. But the only way one can tell whether this seed of faith is alive is for it to grow and to bring forth fruit. By your profession you have said that your life is ingrafted in Christ. The only way one can tell whether a branch is truly grafted into the vine is for the branch to grow."

This period of waiting is the church's way of saying that growth is not optional. Growth is essential. The current "loss" within the membership of the church cannot be allowed to continue. It is a sin against those who are thus "won"—and, perhaps, deceived. The church cannot rely exclusively on a "profession" as the *sole evidence* of one's salvation. Its validity can be demonstrated in obedience.

The present status of religion in society and in the life of the churches is another reason a period of waiting is necessary. Many recognize the necessity of a period of waiting on our mission fields because time is needed for those who come out of a pagan background to give evidence that they have an understanding of and a commitment to the Christian way. But, so the argument goes, the ones who have grown up in the church and in "Christian America" already understand what it means to be a Christian. But what kind of religion do we have in "Christian America"? A recent survey indicated that 99 per cent of the population believe in God. In what kind of God do Americans believe? There are numerous indications that he is not the God of the Scriptures. Over 60 per cent of our population are affiliated with some church. It is popular to be religious. It is good business to be religious. But what is the nature of this religion?

The very "religiousness" of our culture is a serious handicap to the church in seeking to recapture the true vitality of the Christian faith. The early church developed in a culture that was highly "religious." "The climate of opinion then, like our own at the present time, was pro-religion and precisely for that reason was emphatically anti-Christian." [*] A person growing up in modern "religious" America does not necessarily come to understand the true nature and meaning of the Christian life. Rather, quite the opposite would more likely be the outcome. He might easily get a distorted and inadequate concept of the Christian faith.

When we turn to the church, the argument that those growing up in the church would not need a period of waiting would be valid if the life lived by the church were a true demonstration of New Testament Christianity. However, if the Christian life is understood in terms of undertaking a mission and fulfilling a ministry for God in the world, then the life lived by a majority of the present-day church members is such a shallow, superficial representation as almost to be called "pseudo religion."

Again, it must be said that there is nothing wrong with the preaching that has been done in this area. The person who

[*] Perry, *op. cit.*, p. 2.

contemplates becoming a Christian hears the preacher speak of "laying one's life on the altar," "surrendering one's life completely," "taking up one's cross," and "sacrificing all for Christ." But when he tries to understand the nature of the Christian life he will be expected to live, he looks around him at the lives of the church members. From them he learns that he is to be moral, to attend church, and perhaps to tithe. He hears talk of the need for sacrifice, but he sees no serious sacrifice being made. He hears about God's redemptive mission, but he does not see the membership seriously undertaking this mission. He hears talk about taking up the cross, but he does not see the membership carrying any cross by challenging some evil in the world to give their witness to God. All that seems to be expected is for him to be a decently respectable church member.

It is the contention here that a child, youth, or adult living in the midst of this shallow, superficial expression of the Christian life would have as great difficulty coming to understand the demands of God concerning the true nature of the Christian life as a pagan who comes out of heathenism. Indeed, he may have an even greater difficulty because of "reverse psychology." It would be necessary for him to unlearn what he thought was the Christian life, that which he had grown up to believe, before he could come to understand the true nature of Christian discipleship. Thus, in the midst of this situation, a period of waiting is needed to ascertain whether the individual has come to have this understanding of the New Testament view of the Christian life.

This suggests a fourth reason. Because the life lived by the church is such a powerful educative force, the church must strive toward vitality and purity in her life. The influence of the life lived by the church as an educative force has not been adequately understood nor sufficiently emphasized. Although no statistical studies have been made that can be cited to substantiate this claim, it is quite probable that the most powerful teaching force in the entire church is not the pulpit, nor the Sunday school, nor any other educational agency. It is the life lived by the church.

In our framework of democracy with our emphasis on letting everyone decide for himself and on being tolerant because "we are all sinners," this idea that the church must exercise care in maintaining the purity and vitality of her life will seem abhorrent to some. Yet this must be done or else the most powerful teaching force the church has will be negative instead of positive. In fact, this is one of our major problems today. As has been indicated, preachers proclaim in urgent terms the demands of the Christian faith; in Sunday school and in other educational organizations the highest Christian ideals are taught; but these largely fall on deaf ears because the life lived by the church does not demonstrate that it expects these to be put into practice.

It was not so in the early church. Then the life of the church demonstrated to all potential converts the demands of the Christian life. Let us consider, however, the situation of a convert today who has had a genuine saving encounter with God in Christ and has a holy desire to discover and express in his life the deeper meaning of the Christian life. Looking around at the members of the church, he finds most of them, including the leaders, simply "being good" and attending the services. If he suspects that this is not a true expression of the Christian life, and if he seeks to break out of this pattern in his own life, often the church membership lifts its collective eyebrow and views the individual as a fanatic, or at best, a bit odd. Thus, the church may tend to stifle whatever noble and daring impulses the individual might have. If, indeed, these impulses happen to be misdirected, the church does not come to his assistance with guidance in finding a dynamic and challenging expression of these deep and holy impulses. It seems to fear the spiritual adventure.

The life of the modern church stifles rather than encourages daring Christian living, in spite of its preaching and teaching to the contrary. Thus, these impulses eventually die, and the individual settles down simply to being good and attending the services. The church tends to mold the new members in its own image. In doing so, the expression of the Christian life deteriorates into the observance of external forms and the church continues toward institutionalism. If the church is ever going to approach the ideal of a dynamic, experiential faith, it must make sure that its life shall be as accurate an expression of the vitality and purity of the New Testament faith as possible.

Another reason for the waiting period is so obvious that it needs only brief explanation and defense: to insure a regenerate church membership. This reason has two facets to it. First, when there are unregenerate members in the church, it is difficult for the church to give its witness to God and for God, particularly when this witness would challenge the *status quo* about some evil that is accepted by society. Of course, among the regenerate there will be differences of opinion as to what is the "will of God" in controversial matters. But the situation will be made even more difficult with the presence of the unregenerate in the church. Even with differences of opinion, the regenerate seriously *want* to know the will of God and will earnestly search for it that they might express it as their witness. But the unregenerate do not want to know the will of God, and they certainly will not want to express it if it calls for change in their lives. They simply want to let alone and be left alone. If the decision were left to them, the church would do nothing.

The second facet is that with an unregenerate membership the witness of the church to the world is ineffective. The inconsistent lives of its members handicap the witness of the church. This condition has been with us for so long that we accept it as "normal"—and do little about it but complain. To have a waiting period would be one way of seeking to change the situation. Church leaders are deeply concerned over the evident lack of spiritual power and influence on the part of the church. It is "big" but is not having a proportionate influence in changing the world. Christian history indicates that the church has never changed the world by having large numbers of uncommitted members, but rather by small groups who were transformed and transforming. This is a lesson which is difficult for a "successful" religious group to learn. Conner is right in saying that "an unregenerated church cannot be the means of conveying the renewing grace of God to an unregenerate society around it." [7]

A period of waiting is needed, in the sixth place, because our present practice of granting "full membership" to candidates immediately upon their profession of faith, especially young children, actually presents a serious theological problem that has not been faced realistically. Church statistics indicate a rather significant "falling away" from the church during the period of middle adolescence. If one holds the doctrine of "once saved, always saved," what is to be the verdict concerning these who "fall away"? It is true that some of these who leave the church during this period later return. But the fact remains, many do not. What of these? Surely it cannot be said that an individual was saved on the basis of a profession he made when he was a small child, while his whole later life is a denial of any genuine relationship with Christ.

Therefore, it is suggested that all converts should be received first as professing members. If full membership were to be postponed, the individual would have opportunity to give more mature evidence that his commitment to Christ was genuine. Again, it must be remembered that this period of waiting has nothing to do with the individual's salvation. The church is simply saying that it needs some "credible evidence" before the individual is received into full membership.

This is not discrimination against the candidate. The period of waiting would have exactly the opposite effect in practice. This period of waiting would help both the *individual* and the *church* be more aware of the need to make as sure as is humanly possible that this initial experience was genuine and

---

[7] *Op. cit.*, p. 261.

vital. It would also help them recognize the need for diligence in keeping this experience alive and growing. It would serve to bring into sharp focus, both to the individual and church, the importance—even the necessity—of *continuing* in Christ. The very nature of this view suggests that not to continue in Christ brings dire consequences for those who persist in their failure—which is the teaching of the New Testament.

Criterion for Admission

The question inevitably arises: What will be the criterion or standard used for admitting people to full membership? This is a fundamental question, and the answer will largely determine whether this proposal may be used in recapturing experiential religion or whether it would lead to the very thing it is seeking to avoid—institutionalism. In answer to the question, it must be said categorically that the church must not work up a list of external requirements for the candidate to meet. Such requirements would lead inevitably to externalism in religion and to institutionalism in the church.

Rather, the criterion will have to be stated in terms of a general principle. In this we can do no better than to follow the example of Jesus. Jesus did not formulate a code of ethics which he required his followers to obey. He did not tell them what kind of amusements they might safely enjoy. He did not form a detailed creedal statement which they had to accept. He simply said the essence of religion was to love God with all one's being, and to love one's neighbor as oneself. Therefore, the criterion is simply this: *Does the individual give indication that he has a growing understanding of the mission to which he has been called by God, and in his life does he give concrete and observable evidence that he has accepted and is fulfilling this ministry in the world?* The implications of this principle were discussed in some detail in Part II.

This criterion means that both the church and the professing member must have a clear understanding of the biblical view of the Christian life as mission. God calls everyone to the same mission. The church must also have a clear understanding of its ministry, that is, how this mission is to be expressed in the world. Here there may be wide variety because people are different in their interests, vocations, and abilities. The effectiveness of this criterion will be determined by the clarity with which the people of God understand the nature of their calling under God. If this be lacking, the criterion will have no meaning, and the church will have lost the meaning of her existence.

Any standard has dangers. It might become mechanical. It might major on minor negative ethics. It might become legalistic. The question we must face is: Shall we have no standard, no criterion for church membership, or shall we have a criterion that inevitably involves dangers, and then have sufficient confidence in the congregation that it will keep the criterion alive and vital in terms of relevance to the Christian faith? Not to have such faith would imply the inevitability of institutionalism in the life of the church, that is, that the congregation cannot keep clear the essential meaning of her existence. Only a clear understanding of mission and ministry will keep the criterion from becoming legalistic and mechanical.

This period of waiting should apply to candidates of all ages, whether they request membership on a profession of faith or by letter. There should be no specific time limit for this period of waiting. Such a practice might lead to externalism and fail to take account of those dynamic factors at work in this period of waiting. For example, one man applies for membership by letter. He was a respected leader in another church. He continues his ministry in the community into which he has moved. He might be ready to be received into full membership in two months. Another who applies for membership by letter may not be known by the congregation or may not have been active in the church from which he came. Full membership might be delayed for a year or longer. While an adult might make a profession of faith and be received into full membership in eight months, it might be best for a young convert to wait for two or three years.

This practice depends in part upon whether the church truly believes in a regenerate church membership and whether it is going to strive seriously to have a regenerate membership.

Objections Considered

Of course there are objections to this proposal. One is that a period of waiting was not practiced in New Testament times. Converts were received immediately into the Christian fellowship. "Then they that gladly received his word were baptized: and the same day there were added unto them about three thousand souls. . . . And the Lord added to the church daily such as should be saved" (Acts 2:41-47). There was no period of waiting for them. They were received into the fellowship and were baptized after a simple confession of faith, "Jesus Christ is Lord."

But let us take a closer look at the setting in which this confession of faith was made. For a Jew to confess that Jesus Christ was Lord meant to the religious leaders of that time that he was forsaking the religion of his fathers. Thus, he was "put out of the syngogue." So far as his former religion was concerned, he was excommunicated and condemned to eternal punishment. In many instances he was disowned and disinherited by his family. He was ostracized by society and forsaken by his former friends. If he was in business he was boycotted by faithful Jews, or if he was a laborer, no orthodox Jew would hire him. Thus, his means of livelihood was taken from him. This is a possible reason the early Christians had to sell "their possessions and goods, and parted them to all men, as every man had need" (Acts 2:45).

Faced with the possibility of losing his family and friends, of losing his business or job, no Jew could possibly make the confession that "Jesus Christ is Lord" without having gone through a deep personal struggle. No man was willing to "leave father and mother" to follow a new way unless he was convinced that this new way was the only way. He knew the demands of the Christian life *before* he ever made his confession. Thus, the confession was not so simple and easy after all. No such difficulty or demand faces the candidate today as he contemplates making his profession of faith. Today, joining the church is the thing to do to be successful in business. It's the thing to do to be accepted by society. The situation today is exactly opposite from that which existed in the New Testament.

The fact that a period of waiting was not followed in New Testament times does not make it invalid or unscriptural for our day. Many practices and procedures are followed in our churches which were not practiced in the New Testament period. These are designed, however, to achieve the basic teachings of the New Testament. This period of waiting is designed to accomplish the same purpose. Although it was not practiced in the New Testament, it does have strong support in early Christian history. "Let him who is to be a catechumen be a catechumen for three years; but if any one be diligent, and has a good-will to his business, let him be admitted: for it is not the length of time, but the course of life, that is judged." [8] Hurst observed: "The apostles baptized immediately on the profession [of faith] of Christ, but the Church of the patristic period made the careful training of the candidate for church membership the substitute for immediate baptism." [9]

Whether baptism should be postponed as a part of the entrance of the member into full membership or whether it should be administered as a part of his reception as a professing member is still an open question. The answer should be determined on the basis of what is the real meaning and significance of baptism. [10] Further study needs to be done in this

---

[8] A. Roberts and J. Donaldson (eds.), *The Ante-Nicene Fathers* (New York: Charles Scribner's Sons, 1886), VII, 495.

[9] *Op. cit.*, p. 342.

[10] Cf. White, *The Biblical Doctrine of Initiation.*

area. However, the fact that a waiting period was not observed in the New Testament does not seem to be a valid objection. If this practice is in harmony with and is designed to achieve the basic purposes of the New Testament, and if it does not contradict any principle of the New Testament, it is valid.

Some object to the period of waiting on the basis that the Scriptures forbid us to "judge," citing the passage, "Judge not, that ye be not judged. For with what judgment ye judge, ye shall be judged: and with what measure ye mete, it shall be measured to you again" (Matt. 7:1-2). When properly understood, however, this passage does not forbid or contradict the practice being proposed. There is a play on verb tenses in this passage. Thus, a paraphrase might read, "Do not make a practice of judging," or "Don't persist in judging," or "Don't be perpetually censorious" (present tense, linear action), "in order that the judgment of God may not fall on you for an instant" (aorist tense, point action), "because God will judge the standards by which you judge." That is, if faulty human elements such as pride and jealousy enter into your judgment, you will be judged for these faults. Thus, this passage is a warning against setting up external standards which people are required to meet.

Actually this seventh chapter of Matthew is a good chapter to defend the necessity for judging. In at least two instances the necessity for judging others is implied. "Give not that which is holy unto the dogs, neither cast ye your pearls before swine" (Matt. 7:6). Here it is necessary to judge who are the "dogs" and the "swine." Again, "Beware of false prophets, which come to you in sheep's clothing, but inwardly they are ravening wolves" (Matt. 7:15). Here it is necessary to judge who are the false prophets. They come in "sheep's clothing." They may even make a profession of faith. How can we tell who they are? What shall be the basis of our judgment? In the next verse we find Jesus' answer: "Ye shall know them by their fruits" (Matt. 7:16). This involves judgment. Thus, rather than prohibiting judging, this passage, emphasizes the necessity for judging, with a warning not to judge on a human basis but on the basis of divine standards for which even we must be willing to stand judgment.

It must be recognized that we, too, are sinners and that we must stand beside the unbeliever or the professing member and cry with him, "God be merciful to us sinners." On other occasions Jesus commanded the Christian to judge (Matt. 16:6). Paul certainly expected the church to judge (1 Cor. 5:1-7). We feel that it is perfectly proper for judgment to be made on the mission fields. We must conclude, then, that this objection is not valid. Surely the church can determine whether a certain individual shall have the sanction of the church as a representative of Jesus Christ. It has both the right and the responsibility to do this. The church must exercise some type of careful judgment in receiving people into its membership, or else the doctrine of a regenerate church membership becomes a farce.

Others object to this period of waiting, saying, "Salvation is such an intensely personal matter, it should not be questioned." In reply, it must be stated that this period of waiting has nothing to do with the individual's salvation. That is, the church is not judging whether he is saved or not. If there were any question as to his salvation, he would not even be received as a professing member! However, the extreme individualism that claims that only the individual knows whether he is saved and that he thus should be received directly into the church on the basis of his profession is only partially true. It is true that one enters into a saving relationship only on the basis of a personal, responsible encounter with God through Christ, but when he makes application to become a part of the local church, this is more than an individual matter. This is a concern of the total fellowship. The witness the church gives to the world is involved in its action.

Those who are concerned that they may "keep some saved person out" seemingly have no corresponding fear that they will let some unsaved person in. Recognizing that we are men and not God and thus that we cannot finally know who is truly saved or truly lost, I am convinced that God is going to hold us responsible for the large number of unsaved people we have let into our churches. By so doing we have led them into a false hope. In the final judgment they will stand condemned before God! They trusted the church to give them proper and accurate guidance, and the church deceived them! The kindest thing the church could have done was to make them aware of their true condition before God that they might have been led to repentance and into a genuine saving relationship with God.

Another objection, closely related to the above, will need only brief reply since it has been answered indirectly. Some argue that we cannot tell with any degree of certainty who is regenerate and who is not. W. T. Conner answered this argument a number of years ago: "We do not maintain that the ideal in the matter can be perfectly attained. Of course, there have been some unregenerated people in the churches and always will be, no doubt, but this does not prove the doctrine wrong. It only proves the necessity of guarding the more carefully the membership of the churches." [11]

Some object that those who are received as professing members will not feel completely a part of the fellowship. This objection should be viewed from two perspectives. First, it must be recognized that they are not completely a part of the fellowship. On the other hand, if the church seriously accepts its responsibility to these professing members, it would have exactly the opposite effect. The present practice of receiving them immediately into full membership certainly does not guarantee that they have come into a fellowship of concern. The large number of nonresident, unreached, unenlisted, and undeveloped church members is proof of this fact. Second, this period of waiting would serve as a constant reminder to the church that its primary task to these who had made a profession was to throw its arms of fellowship and concern about

---

[11] *Op. cit.*, p. 261.

them and provide both the stimulus and opportunity for growth toward an understanding of their mission and ministry in the world as Christians.

Perhaps the most serious objection to this proposal arises because of the practical difficulties involved in seeking to implement it in the life of the churches. "To do this would tear our church apart," some would say. Of course the difficulties would be serious, but is not this just the point? In our generation we have admitted such men as "the rich young ruler" to membership and given them a position on the finance committee. Other leading citizens of the community are also members of the church. It is large and successful, but we complain bitterly because we do not have spiritual power.

Can it be that at the peak of our success we are also descending into a desert of lifeless form of religion in our churches? Institutionalism is not a theoretical or academic problem. Even now we cannot think seriously of seeking a regenerate church membership for fear of offending some in our midst or of disrupting our program.

Our survey of the religous movements of history indicates that we stand at a crucial and dangerous period in the cycle that leads to institutionalism. To seek to maintain the *status quo* to follow the course of expediency, to walk the path others have trod is only to complete the cycle. The purposes of God will not be thwarted. He will raise up a people with experiential faith. However, if we are going to break the pattern, if we are going to seek to exercise purposive control in the movement of which we are a part, if we are going to seek to recapture this experiential faith, then drastic action is needed. This proposal for a period of waiting could be a disruptive force in the life of our churches. It could also be disturbing if we were to insist on an understanding of the Christian life as mission and ministry. Many would be upset if in our evangelism we were to insist on a deeper understanding of the nature of authentic faith. Being disrupted may be a part of the price we must pay to recapture experiential faith. By every means possible we will want to keep this disruption at a minimum, but nothing must deter us from the basic objective.

How to Get Started

If a church seriously contemplates implementing this proposal it will immediately face a perplexing problem. How to get started? This is not easy to answer. Getting started will be complicated by the fact that already within the church's membership are many who by their indifference and by their practice in life give no evidence that they are regenerate. They will surely rise up in protest at such a suggestion because this makes them call into question a relationship that they thought was "sealed." But if the church is genuinely interested in them and concerned about them, this proposal is the best thing that the church could do for them. Nevertheless, this unregenerate element in the church will present a far more difficult situation in which to seek a regenerate church membership than if the church were starting *de novo*.

The problem of getting started is further compounded by the fact that most church members—even the leaders—do not have enough understanding of the nature of the Christian life and the essential mission of the people of God in the world to see why a regenerate church membership is such an impelling necessity. Lacking this understanding they will tend to resist any and all changes that might create a disturbance in the church. They will also be sensitive as to how this will affect the financial program of the church. Their natural inclination will be to go along with what we are now doing. If this is true of the inner circle leadership, how much more intense will be the problem among those who are on the fringe of the life of the church?

Thus, the place to start is with the present church membership. In getting started we will need to observe first the principle of understanding. Our first task will be to seek to give our members that information and guidance which will lead them into a deeper understanding of the meaning of and need for a regenerate church membership. Start with the inner circle of leadership, those who will most likely understand. In private conversations and small group meetings discuss the matters pertaining to this problem—what it means to be a Christian, how one becomes a Christian, what it means to be the people of God. It is hoped that this book might serve as a basis for study and discussion in these small study groups. In time enlarge these conversations and meetings to include other church leaders. Then seek to get the essential information to the total church membership through sermons, articles, and discussion in regular meetings.

Second, we will need to observe the principle of patience. That is, in implementing this proposal we will need to proceed slowly and make changes gradually. An infinite amount of patience will be needed in guiding the people. On the other hand, persistent pressure will need to be kept on the people to effect needed changes. Because of the difficulties inherent in the problem, the inclination of most leaders will be to make no changes at all.

Unless we are content to go on as we now are and receive members merely on the basis of a profession of faith and let the doctrine of a regenerate church membership mean nothing in the life and fellowship of the church, we have no other alternative but to accept the risks and the difficulties involved in postponing church membership. At all costs the criterion must be kept spiritual in terms of the essential nature of the Christian life. *In the final analysis, it is the clarity with which the people of God see and understand their mission for God in the world and the manner in which they interpret and implement that mission that is decisive.*

If not a period of waiting, how shall we go about the task of seeking to achieve the ideal of a regenerate church membership, insofar as this is humanly possible? How shall we seek to insure that ours is truly the "gathered church," or more correctly, the "dispersed church"? How shall we seek to make sure that the church is in fact the "people of God," the "remnant," the "body of Christ"? How shall we teach the people that the church is not a building to which people come, but a fellowship of obedient believers in Christ who have a mission and who have committed themselves to the ministry of fulfilling this mission? It may be difficult to change the program of the churches, but if what has been said is biblically sound, and if our interpretation of the implications of this theology is correct, then our program must change!

12

Christian Discipline and
a Regenerate Church Membership

The second major innovation that will be necessary in the life of the church if we are to approach the ideal of a regenerate church member involves the practice of Christian discipline. The pattern of church life that has the best possibility of leading to an experimental faith begins to emerge more clearly now. It has been stated previously that in a saving encounter the individual must respond to God in terms of the mission for which God calls him as a Christian. It has also been stated that growth toward and into this mission is not optional. In addition, in the strict sense, it is not possible for one to have a saved soul and a lost life. Man is a unity and when he is saved, he is saved in the totality of his being. When these factors are kept in focus, it is clear that the disciple must submit himself to the discipline of the Christian life as a necessary part of the total salvation experience. This is *not* salvation by works. What is done for the individual is done by God alone. But this emphasis does say something exceedingly important about the *quality* of the saving relationship. This is an emphasis which the modern church has not kept in focus.

Why Christian Discipline Is Not Practiced

The typical church member of today views church discipline simply as a puritanical appendage of early church life in the United States which fortunately has been discarded. In our "enlightened" age of tolerance such a practice would be unthinkable. However, the practice has not been discarded because the church has become so pure in life and doctrine that it is no longer needed. Rather, it has been discarded for exactly the opposite reasons. Four are mentioned. First, sin is so prevalent in the lives of the members that the church does not know where to start. Faced with the magnitude of the task and the difficulties involved, the members begin piously to say, "We are all sinners"; "Let him that is without sin cast the first stone"; "Judge not that ye be not judged." The difficulty with this point of view is that the clear teaching of the New Testament indicates that we *are* to judge! It cautions that extreme care must be exercised as to *how* we judge. It is true, however, that the lives of most church members are of such nature that inaugurating Christian displine will be an exceedingly difficult task.

A second and closely related reason is that the practice of church discipline would be a major disruptive force in the life of the church. Some of the leading members in the church and some of the most influential people in the community might be involved. The leadership of the church is sensitive to the fact that the church debt must be paid. Gifts to world mission causes must not be jeopardized. Nothing must be done that will create dissension. Writing in this area to the specific needs of his own communion, one author poses a question that we also might ponder: "Is there any conceivable circumstance in which the Reformed Church will take any disciplinary action against anyone with an income of over $10,000 a year? Or may one spit on the open Bible with impunity?"[1] It may be that this "disruption" is a part of the "cross" the church must accept if she is to recapture experiential religion.

In the third place, there has been a positive revolt against the flagrant abuses that have often attended the practice of church discipline. Christian history is replete with instance after instance of discipline that was practiced in the name

---

[1] Geddes MacGregor, *The Coming Reformation* (Philadelphia: The Westminster Press, 1960), p. 82.

of Christ but was really erroneous, unjust, and unchristian. Wrongly understood and practiced, discipline has been one of the devil's most powerful and effective weapons in bringing shame upon the Christian enterprise. This danger must be faced realistically.

A fourth factor that has contributed to the loss of discipline in the modern church, and perhaps underlying all the others, is that church members today have a low view of what it means to be the church. We do not even approach a realistic understanding of what the New Testament means by being the people of God. As one student put it, the most surprising aspect of the contemporary picture is that "we as Southern Baptists, with our 'largeness,' seem to have found less need for the practice of discipline than the much smaller community of the New Testament." The difference is that the New Testament community had a high view of what it meant to be the body of Christ, the people of God.

Discipline in the New Testament

The practice of Christian discipline has a firm foundation in the teachings of the New Testament. All of the passages that emphasize Christian growth and development are related to the "developmental" aspect of discipline. In addition, there are several passages that specifically deal with discipline in its "corrective" form. In Matthew 18:15-17 Jesus spoke to the problem. In this, the second recorded instance in which he referred to the "church," he indicated the procedure the Christian is to follow in seeking reconciliation with a brother who has trespassed against him. If the brother persistently refused to be reconciled after every effort had been made in that direction, Jesus counseled: "Let him be unto thee as an heathen man and a publican" (v. 17).

The apostle Paul in a letter to the Corinthian church dealt with the problem of a member who was evidently living with his father's wife (1 Cor. 5:1-13). He vigorously reproved the church for its failure to take action in this instance. He stated that, although he was not present, he had already judged the man. He then admonished them when they were assembled "to deliver such an one unto Satan for the destruction of the flesh" (v. 5). This discipline was to serve two purposes. The first had to do with the welfare of the man himself, that his "spirit may be saved" (v. 5). The second had to do with the purity of the church (vv. 7-8).

In 2 Thessalonians 3:6-15 Paul again instructed a church to deal with certain misguided brethren in terms of admonition. In his first letter to Timothy, Paul dealt with the problem of discipline as it related to doctrinal issues (1 Tim. 6:3-5). Some may interpret this as counsel to Timothy as an individual, that he should "withdraw himself" from the man who is "proud, knowing nothing, but doting about questions and strifes of words" (v. 4). But if this withdrawing is necessary for Timothy as an individual, how much more important it would be for the church to do the same since it would not be as "strong in the faith" as Timothy.

The problem of correct doctrine was faced in 2 John 9-11. The question concerned those who "abideth not in the doctrine of Christ" (v. 9). The Elder wrote, "receive him not into your house, neither bid him God speed" (v. 10); for any who bids such a one "God speed is partaker of his evil deeds" (v. 11). Again the question arises as to whether this is individual counsel or spoken to a church. It seems likely that the "elect lady" (v. 1) refers to a church. But even if it applies to an individual, the argument given above in the case of Timothy is applicable here.

It is, indeed, surprising to discover the number of passages in the New Testament that refer to Christian discipline. Many of our other doctrines and practices have much less biblical basis. Some people have built a whole system of eschatology with little more than Revelation 20:3-7 as the foundation. We give deacons a central responsibility in the life of our churches on the basis of a few verses of Scripture. Even the practice of ordination has limited references in Scripture. Yet with the abundance of Scripture related to discipline, we still calmly ignore it.

Discipline also has a firm foundation in Baptist history. It has always been 'closely related to the faith and life of the church. Thus "in early Baptist circles, . . . 'confessions of faith' and 'abstracts of discipline' were usually published in a single volume." [2] There are two types of Christian discipline: "formative discipline," which places primary emphasis on teaching and training, and "reformative discipline," which seeks to care for a brother who has been overtaken in a fault and is more corrective in nature.

Perhaps the major weakness of discipline in its practice throughout most of history was that it tended to major on the reformative or punitive aspect. Too often it was concerned with negative ethics in terms of a legalistic norm. Also its primary purpose was not always redemptive. The church did not feel with, share with, confess with, and continue to show loving concern for the one who was disciplined. The corrective aspect of discipline is important, but the church must understand that it is certainly not the whole of discipline.

Formative Discipline

"Discipline" and "disciple" come from the same root word and in its basic meaning "discipline" refers to "the instruction or training given to a disciple or learner." [3] Thus, formative church discipline is that process of teaching and training by which the Christian is increasingly formed in the image of Christ. The purity of the church, as important as this is, is not the primary purpose underlying discipline. The fundamental purposes of discipline relate to the work of God in the world and the welfare of the individual. Littell puts it this way: "The Church does not accent discipline for its own sake, but because

---

[2] Theron D. Price, "Discipline in the Church," in *What Is the Church?* ed. Duke K. McCall (Nashville: Broadman Press, 1958), p. 165.

[3] Gaines S. Dobbins, *The Churchbook* (Nashville: Broadman Press, 1951), p. 85.

it is the Lord's will that his people be armed as well as possible for the spiritual battle."[4]

In Christian nurture the disciple subjects himself to the discipline of Christ. This process is lifelong in scope and is not optional in nature. The purpose of this discipline is to equip the individual to fulfil the mission for which he was called as a Christian. Formative discipline is exercised in the Christian community as the members express genuine concern for one another and become dynamically involved with one another in deep interpersonal relationships, recognizing that they all are held accountable by God for their stewardship of life. Its purpose is to enlighten, encourage, stimulate, support, and sustain one another and the group in the discipline under which they live and in the fulfilment of their divine mission.

In formative discipline both the individual and the church have a responsibility. The individual has a responsibility to enter into the transforming relationship with Christ in which the motive—the impelling desire—for growth is present. The church does not supply the individual with this desire to grow, but the church is responsible for seeking to provide those conditions in which the individual is encouraged to enter into a genuine encounter with Christ. It is from this encounter that the motive must come, not from any program or technique devised by the church. For this reason strong emphasis was placed on an adequate understanding of the nature of authentic faith. Also for this reason did we stress the necessity for a conscious, voluntary choice—a conversion experience.

Too often the church has been undertaking an impossible task. It has been trying to make people act as Christians when they have not really had this transforming experience with Christ in which they were made over into "new creatures." Thus, the church has resorted to every kind of "gimmick" and stimulus to try to motivate and induce people to live the Christian life. It is not *natural* for a person to love his enemy or even to love his neighbor as himself. No "gimmick" can

[4] F. H. Littell, *The Free Church* (Boston: Starr King Press, 1957), p. 131.

lead him to do this—only the transforming work of Christ. Whether the individual responds to this radical call of God is his responsibility.

It is the responsibility of the church to provide the individual with the fellowship and the conditions in which he may become a "disciple" of Christ and thus submit himself to the "discipline" of the Christian way. How this may best be done can ultimately be determined on the basis of careful study, sharing experiences, and practical experimentation.[5]

The professing member, indeed every regenerate member, ought to be related to the church in its organizational life. It is through this fellowship, Bible study, and training that he can be stimulated to grow and become better equipped to give his witness in the world as an instrument in God's redemptive purpose. This does not mean that the individual must spend all his time going to meetings so that he has neither the time nor the incentive to give his witness in the world. It simply means that the individual cannot grow apart from the Christian fellowship, and this fellowship must have some type of organizational structure to accomplish certain ends. The individual's devotion and loyalty to Christ would not be determined by the number of meetings he attends but rather by *what he does in the world.* The success of an organization or meeting would not be determined by the number it had in attendance but rather by what happens in the lives of those who attend and by *what they do in the world.* Thus the total program of the church is involved in this formative discipline.[6]

In addition, I propose a special class for new professing members. This proposal is certainly not new. Many churches

---

[5] The Baptist Sunday School Board has set up a "New Member Program" in the Training Union Department to give special emphasis to this phase of church life. An intensive study is now under way to discover the best ways of caring for and ministering to new church members. This is a most encouraging and significant development.

[6] There is an excellent discussion of the value and use of (1) Sunday school classes, (2) inquirer's classes, (3) person-centered groups, and (4) individual pastoral care in *Pastoral Evangelism* by Samuel Southard (Nashville: Broadman Press, 1962), pp. 105-130.

already have such a class for new members. Most of the current courses are inadequate, however, both in the curriculum offered and in the amount of time given to the study. The majority of these courses last for four Sundays and generally deal with such topics as: (1) the significance of the decision the convert has made, (2) Baptist doctrines, (3) the program of the local church, and (4) the program of the denomination. As fundamental as these topics are, they are not adequate for the kind of study the professing member needs. This course of study seems to be designed primarily to enable the individual to become a good "church member" rather than a good Christian. It is entirely possible for one to become a co-operating member of the organizational life of the church and never fulfil his ministry for God in the world. In addition, the time given to this study is altogether inadequate even to begin to do what the professing member needs.

For this reason, it is proposed that the course of study for this special class should last for one year. The course would be built around units of study which, on the average, would last for four Sundays each. This would, of course, have to be flexible, for some units might last for only three or even two Sundays while other units might last for five or six Sundays. A possible course of study might include:

1. The nature of the salvation experience
2. The nature of the mission to which the Christian is called
3. The Christian's personal spiritual development
4. The Christian's ministry in the world
5. The Christian as a witness in business
6. The Christian as a witness in family relations
7. The Christian as a witness in society
8. The program of the local church
9. The program of the denomination
10. Baptist doctrines
11. The history of the church
12. The history of Baptists

In determining the curriculum, the needs of the new convert must be kept constantly in mind. What can be done to help him understand more fully the significance of the experience he has had with Christ? What can be done that will serve best to get him properly introduced to the discipline of the new life "in Christ"? Even in a year no adequate study of any of these areas can be made in any detail. The purpose of this study, however, is to take the professing member at the time when the warm zeal of his experience with Christ is deep within him and *introduce* him to those major areas where his Christian life is to be developed and expressed. Study in other groups at a later time will provide opportunity for further study in depth in these and other areas as this formative discipline continues throughout life.

Several practical problems inhere in this proposal. For example, what is done about the person who makes his profession of faith at a time of the year when the special class is in the middle of this study? Is it better for him to enter the class and perhaps be overwhelmed by his lack of background? Or is it better for him to wait for the next class and perhaps risk losing some of his initial zeal? Is there some other alternative? Obviously, it is better for such a class to be graded so that the children, youth, and adults can better have their special needs met. Can this grading be done in a small church? Who should teach the class? Should it be the pastor? Should other church members be trained to teach certain areas of the study? When is the best time for the class to meet? If this proposal is sound, experience will enable us to find answers to these questions.

Should this course of study be required? Normally most of the professing members will enter this course of study. But because individuals vary so widely both in their needs and in their previous development, this should not be made a requirement. This tends toward legalism. There are many other ways an individual may give evidence that he has a growing understanding of the mission for which he was called as a Christian and give evidence of his commitment to it. A professing member may choose, for some adequate reason, not to complete the entire year of study. He may choose to relate himself to some other study group in the life of the church that would more adequately meet his particular needs. By the same token, it is not assumed that a person will automatically be voted into full membership after completing this year of study. Rigidity and legalistic requirements must be avoided.

On the other hand, if a professing member does not enter this course of study, if he does not relate himself to any other part of the organized life of the church in which opportunity for study and growth is provided, if in no other way does he give evidence that he has an understanding of that for which he was called as a Christian, then it is the responsibility of the church to exercise urgent and concerned admonition in behalf of the individual. If he is adamant and persists in this refusal, it becomes the responsibility of the church, for the welfare of the individual, to recognize that he has rejected the fellowship of the church. Thus he would be dropped as a professing member. The church would continue to demonstrate loving concern for him in seeking to woo and win him. But he must be led to face frankly his need.

The more effective the church is in carrying out this formative discipline, the less necessary it will be for the church to exercise discipline in its reformative aspects. This is one of the reasons that a period of waiting is a fundamental necessity in the life of our churches. It can dramatically focus the attention of both the church and the individual on the fact that growth and development under the discipline of Christ is not simply desirable but imperative! Indeed, in our approach to evangelism the prospective candidate should be made aware of this disciplined discipleship to which he is to subject himself *before* he makes his profession of faith.

Reformative Discipline

Because our best efforts at formative discipline will be imperfect, because the best human judgment is not infallible, and most of all because human nature is as it is, the church must also exercise reformative discipline. Sometimes called corrective discipline, it consists of the efforts of the church to deal with an erring brother. It is the church seeking to encourage and assist a brother to re-form his life which has become marred. In the early church two major factors made necessary the exercise of reformative or corrective discipline, namely, sin or moral lapse (Matt. 18:15-19; 1 Cor. 5:1-13; 2 Cor. 2:4-8) and heretical teaching that subverted the truth and threatened the fellowship (1 Tim. 6:3-5; 2 Tim. 2:16-18; Titus 3:10-11).

Historically, reformative discipline has been a fundamental part of Baptist church life. In the second edition (1813) of the *Charleston Confession of Faith* there was included in an appendix "A Treatise on Church Discipline, with a Variety of Forms." W. L. Lumpkin concludes that in the South this Confession "influenced Baptist thought generally and has been perhaps the most influential of all confessions. Local church covenants still reflect its outlook and summarize its doctrines."[7] It outlines three levels of church censure, depending on the severity of the offense, namely, rebuke or admonition, suspension, and excommunication.

"Rebuke or admonition, the lowest degree of church censure, is reproving an offender, pointing out the offense, charging it upon the conscience, advising and exhorting him to repentance, watchfulness, and new obedience, and praying for him that he may be reclaimed (Titus 1:13)."[8] This level of discipline was to be exercised for such matters as causing a weaker brother to stumble by engaging in matters which in themselves were indifferent, or if he were contentious about minor matters, or if he neglected "privately to admonish or reprove a brother whom he knows to be guilty of sin (Lev. 19:17)."[9] Thus the failure to exercise proper discipline, itself, was to be disciplined.

[7] *Op. cit.*, p. 352.
[8] James Leo Garrett, Jr., *Baptist Church Discipline* (Nashville: Broadman Press, 1962), p. 42.
[9] *Ibid.*, p. 43.

"Suspension, considered as a church censure, is that act of a church whereby an offending member, being found guilty, is set aside from office, from the Lord's table, and from the liberty of judging or voting in any case." In this level of discipline the brother was "not cut off from union, but only from communion with the church." He certainly was not to be viewed as an "enemy" but as rather to be "admonished as a brother," and upon a "credible profession of repentance," the censure was to be lifted and the brother "restored to all the privileges of the church." [10] This type of discipline should be exercised for such matters as a brother's withdrawing himself from the church because of "its wholesome discipline" in spite of all admonitions, or if he began to teach heretical views, or if there was a serious lapse in his moral life. If a person was guilty of some gross crime but gave evidence of sincere repentance, he was to be suspended until the matter could be investigated. "In a word, all practices that in their own nature and tendency are destructive of the reputation, peace, and prosperity of the church and yet appear not to be past remedy merit this censure." [11] In other words, the church must be seriously concerned about (1) the welfare of its own fellowship, (2) the purity of its life, and (3) the witness it gives to the world.

"Excommunication is a censure of the highest degree; it is a judicial act of the church in which, by the authority of Christ, she cuts off and entirely excludes an unworthy member from union and communion with the church and from all the rights and privileges thereof." [12] Excommunication had to do only with the individual's relation with the church. It did *not* affect the person's salvation. This was a matter only God determined. Also, the church had no authority by which it could assess either personal or civil punishment to the person, such as whippings, imprisonments, or fines, and certainly it could not

[10] *Ibid.*
[11] *Ibid.*, p. 44.
[12] *Ibid.*

assess the punishment of death. This was a gross error made by the church in the past.

In fact, according to this Treatise, the offender was not barred from attending the services of the church where he could hear the preaching and teaching of the Word. This level of discipline was to be used against "(1) all sins that are against the letter of the Ten Commandments . . . (2) all that call for severe corporal punishment from human laws; provided those laws are not contrary to the laws of God . . . (3) all such sins as are highly scandalous in their nature and expose the church to contempt." [13] The responsibility for exercising this disciplinary action always rested in the hands of the congregation and never with any individual or special group.

This historical evidence is not cited as proof that this practice is right. Just because a procedure was followed in the past, however ancient the precedent, does not prove that it is sound and should be followed in the modern church. Rather, this evidence is cited primarily to point out that the proposal being made here is not an innovation but is in harmony with Baptist history.

Numerous factors entered into the discarding of the practice of reformative discipline. It was sorely misused and abused. It was exceedingly difficult to implement. However, "the relaxation of discipline has often more absurd results than ever attended its excess." [14] The abuses we can reject; the difficulties in implementation we can admit; but the principle of discipline remains a valid teaching of the New Testament. The practice of this principle is ignored in the life of the church at the peril of experiential religion. It is now our task to explore, if only in brief, why the proper practice of discipline must be reclaimed by the church.

Many of the reasons given in defense of a period of waiting preceding full membership are also applicable here. For example, the church must be concerned about the purity of her

---

[13] *Ibid.*, p. 45.
[14] MacGregor, *op. cit.*, p. 17.

own life. It must also be concerned about the witness which the life of the church gives to the community. In addition to these, the church must practice discipline because of what the church is as the body of Christ. That is, the church disciplines not in the spirit of vengeance or retribution; rather she disciplines simply by being true to her essential nature. God exercises discipline (judgment), not by meting out judgments, but by being true to his essential nature. God is holy; thus by being true to his essential nature, he is judgment upon man in his unholiness. God is *agape*-love, and thus he is judgment upon man in his self-love. Because God is always consistent in his nature and cannot be other, he is always judgment upon all that is inconsistent with his nature.

Thus, if the church is distinctive in nature, then as it is consistent with that nature, it is judgment upon all that is inconsistent with its nature. Light is always judgment upon darkness. Good is always judgment upon evil. For this reason, the church fails to exercise its disciplinary function only by being untrue to its essential nature.

Some may object to this position. They would remind us that the church is a fellowship of sinners who themselves are striving and have not yet arrived. Those in the church are not perfect as God is perfect. Thus, they say, "Who are we to exercise discipline upon others who are sinners the same as we?" This is just the point. In the final analysis we don't exercise discipline; discipline comes about because we *are* something. Surely we are sinners. But we are sinners saved by grace. We are supposed to be "born again" sinners. We are supposed to have been made over into "new creatures" by the transforming power of God. God has called us to be "a peculiar people." What is this "peculiarity" that is supposed to be characteristic of the people of God? Does the church have no *distinctive* nature? If it does, then as it is consistent with that nature, it inevitably disciplines (is judgment upon) all that is inconsistent with that nature. In the final analysis, the individual brings discipline upon himself. It is he who breaks the fellowship at whatever the point and to whatever degree. The church simply remains consistent with its nature.

The practice of discipline must be reclaimed because, oddly enough, this is one of the best ways the church has of showing *genuine* concern for its own membership. It must be remembered that the purpose of reformative discipline is always redemptive and not primarily punitive (1 Cor. 5:5). It may be that a Christian brother whom the church is seeking to admonish or rebuke will resist the love of the church just as he may resist the love of God. Nevertheless the church must continue to love and to woo him just as God continued to love and to woo us "while we were yet sinners." Or, if by the persistent patterns of a person's life he gives indication that he is not in reality "in Christ," then the church must continue to seek him for redemption with the same urgency and loving concern it would have for any one who is "out of Christ."

A basic responsibility which the church has to any individual, whether he is a brother "in Christ" who has fallen into sin or whether he is one who has demonstrated that he is not "in Christ," is to help him become aware of his true condition. Neither reformation nor redemption can come until he has this awareness. In this area the church is committing serious sin against its own by not exercising discipline. Numerous people within the membership of the churches are living in gross sin. Their lives need re-forming. But the church by its silence permits these people to live with a false view of themselves. These people have conditioned themselves to the preaching and teaching they hear. These things do not disturb them. Therefore, something more radical needs to be done to enable them to become aware of their true condition.

In addition, there are other members of the churches who by their lives give rather conclusive evidence that they have never truly been "born again." Yet they are members of the church. They made their "profession." They have been taught: "once saved, always saved." They are complacent and unconcerned. But from all human indications they are living in a *false hope!*

The kindest thing the church could do for these would be to startle them, if necessary, into an awareness of their true condition. The church through its discipline seeks to lead its members to have this awareness. *By failing to practice discipline, the church is admitting that it does not love its own enough to go through the painful process of seeking their reclamation.*

Among other things, pride and polite respectability have superseded righteousness in the life of the modern churches. Pride over the success we have enjoyed in numerical and monetary increases has become such a dominant factor in the life of our churches that we will allow nothing to be done that might threaten the unity, and thus the success, of our churches. Also our polite respectability would be seriously offended if one were to be brought before the church for discipline. But in this failure to exercise discipline the church simply indicates that it is more deeply concerned over its own success and its own polite respectability than it is over the welfare of its members and the witness the church gives to the world.

Thus, although it is always painful, discipline is just as necessary in the life of a church as it is in the life of a growing child. The parent who permits a child to grow up in unbridled freedom is not the parent who demonstrates the deepest love for the child. Discipline is one of the highest expressions of love. "Whom the Lord loveth he chasteneth" (Heb. 12:6). "As many as I love, I rebuke and chasten: be zealous therefore, and repent" (Rev. 3:19). Discipline is grounded in love and concern—and this is primarily concern for the offender. The church has concern for its own purity and its witness to the world, but the primary concern is the welfare of the individual. Failure to exercise discipline for erring members does not demonstrate genuine love and concern for them. Rather, this failure demonstrates precisely the opposite—a lack of *genuine* love and concern. It indicates that the church is unwilling to suffer, to go through the painful process of discipline for the sake of an erring member in the hope of reclaiming him for God.

The proposals that have been made are radical in nature. Yet only drastic action can meet the needs of the church in its current condition. Many difficulties and dangers attend these proposals. The criteria for admission to full membership may become legalistic and mechanical. Discipline may degenerate into the enforcement of a negative ethic and puritanical code. *But the only thing that will save the church from these dangers is for it to understand with clarity the nature of its fundamental task.* What does it really mean to be the people of God in the world? If it is the task of the church to be an instrument of God to lead people to become Christian, what does it mean to be Christian? When God calls a person to be Christian, what does he call him to be and do? Only as the church understands clearly the answer to these questions will it understand its essential purpose and task. Only as it knows this will it know and be able to fulfil the meaning of its existence.

Bibliography

ALLEN, CLIFTON J. and HOWSE, W. L. *The Curriculum Guide.* Nashville: Convention Press, 1961.

BAILLIE, D. M. *God Was in Christ.* New York: Charles Scribner's Sons, 1948.

BARTH, KARL. *The Teaching of the Church Regarding Baptism.* London: SCM Press, Ltd., 1948.

BEARD, CHARLES. *The Reformation of the Sixteenth Century in Its Relation to Modern Thought and Knowledge.* London: Constable and Company Ltd., 1833.

BETTENSON, HENRY (ed.). *Documents of the Christian Church.* New York: Oxford University Press, 1947.

BONHOEFFER, DIETRICH. *The Cost of Discipleship.* New York: The Macmillan Co., 1959, second ed.

BRANDON, OWEN. *The Battle for the Soul.* Philadelphia: The Westminster Press, 1959.

BRUNNER, EMIL. *Man in Revolt.* Philadelphia: The Westminster Press, 1947.

BULTMANN, RUDOLF. *Theology of the New Testament.* New York: Charles Scribner's Sons, 1951.

BUSHNELL, HORACE. *Christian Nurture.* New Haven: Yale University Press, 1947.

CHERBONNIER, E. LaB. *Hardness of Heart.* Garden City, N. Y.: Doubleday and Co., Inc., 1955.

COE, GEORGE A. *A Social Theory of Religious Education.* New York: Charles Scribner's Sons, 1917.

——————. *Education in Religion and Morals.* New York: Fleming H. Revell Co., 1904.

CONNER, W. T. *Christian Doctrine.* Nashville: Broadman Press, 1937.

COX, CLAIRE. *The New-Time Religion.* Englewood Cliffs, New Jersey: Prentice-Hall, Inc., 1961.

CUBBERLEY, ELLWOOD P. *The History of Education.* New York: Houghton Mifflin Company, 1920.

CULLY, IRIS V. *The Dynamics of Christian Education.* Philadelphia: The Westminster Press, 1958.

CULLMAN, OSCAR. *Immortality of the Soul or Resurrection of the Dead?* London: The Epworth Press, 1958.

DANBY, HERBERT (ed. and trans.). *The Mishnah.* Oxford: At the Clarendon Press, 1933.

DAVIES, D. R. *Secular Illusion or Christian Realism?* New York: The Macmillan Co., 1949.

DOBBINS, GAINES S. *Building Better Churches.* Nashville: Broadman Press, 1947.

————. *The Churchbook.* Nashville: Broadman Press, 1951.

DODD, C. H. *The Bible Today.* New York: The University Press, 1947.

ECKARDT, A. ROY. *The Surge of Piety in America.* New York: Association Press, 1958.

EDGE, FINDLEY B. *Teaching for Results.* Nashville: Broadman Press, 1956.

ELLIOTT, HARRISON S. *Can Religious Education Be Christian?* New York: The Macmillan Company, 1940.

FARMER, H. H. *Revelation and Religion.* London: Nisbet & Co., Ltd., 1954.

FORELL, GEORGE W. *The Protestant Faith.* Englewood Cliffs, New Jersey: Prentice-Hall, Inc., 1960.

GILMORE, A. (ed.). *Christian Baptism.* Philadelphia: The Judson Press, 1959.

GRAETZ, H. *History of the Jews.* Philadelphia: The Jewish Publication Society of America, 1891.

GRAVES, FRANK PIERREPONT. *A History of Education During the Middle Ages.* New York: The Macmillan Company, 1915.

HENDERLITE, RACHEL. *Forgiveness and Hope.* Richmond: John Knox Press, 1961.

HERBERG, WILL. *Protestant, Catholic, Jew.* Garden City, New York: Doubleday and Co., Inc., 1956.

HEUSS, JOHN. *Our Christian Vocation.* Greenwich: Seabury Press, 1955.

HORTON, WALTER M. *Realistic Theology.* New York: Harper and Bros., 1934.

HOWE, RUEL L. *Man's Need and God's Action.* Greenwich: Seabury Press, 1953.

HURST, JOHN FLETCHER. *History of the Christian Church.* New York: Eaton & Mains, 1897.

HUTCHINSON, PAUL. *The New Ordeal of Christianity*. New York: Association Press, 1957.

JESSOP, T. E., *et. al*. *The Christian Understanding of Man*. London: George Allen & Unwin, Ltd., 1939.

JONES, E. STANLEY. *Conversion*. New York: Abingdon Press, 1959.

KIDD, B. J. *A History of the Church*. Oxford: At the Clarendon Press, 1922.

KIRK, KENNETH E. *The Apostolic Ministry*. London: Hodder and Stoughton, Ltd., 1946.

KRAEMER, HENDRIK. *A Theology of the Laity*. London: Lutterworth Press, 1958.

KURTZ, JOHN HENRY. *Church History*. New York: Funk and Wagnalls Company, 1888.

LIGHTFOOT, J. B. *The Christian Ministry*. London: Macmillan and Co., Ltd., 1901.

LITTELL, F. H. *The Free Church*. Boston: Starr King Press, 1957.

LUMPKIN, WILLIAM L. *Baptist Confessions of Faith*. Philadelphia: The Judson Press, 1959.

McGIFFERT, ARTHUR CUSHMAN. *Protestant Thought Before Kant*. New York: Charles Scribner's Sons, 1911.

McGREGOR, GEDDES. *The Coming Reformation*. Philadelphia: The Westminster Press, 1960.

MANSON, T. W. *Ministry and Priesthood:* Christ's and Ours. London: Epworth Press, 1958.

MARCEL, GABRIEL. *The Mystery of Being*. London: The Harvill Press, Ltd., 1951.

MARTY, MARTIN E. *The New Shape of American Religion*. New York: Harper and Bros., 1958.

MILLER, RANDOLPH C. *Christian Nurture and the Church*. New York: Charles Scribner's Sons, 1961.

MINEAR, PAUL S. *Images of the Church in the New Testament*. Philadelphia: The Westminster Press, 1960.

MONROE, PAUL. *A Text-Book in the History of Education*. New York: The Macmillan Company, 1914.

MOORE, ERNEST CARROLL. *The Story of Instruction*. New York: The Macmillan Company, 1948.

MULLINS, E. Y. *The Axioms of Religion*. Philadelphia: The Griffith & Rowland Press, 1908.

NEWBIGIN, LESSLIE. *Sin and Salvation*. London: SCM Press, Ltd., 1956.

NIEBUHR, REINHOLD. *The Nature and Destiny of Man*. New York: Charles Scribner's Sons, 1943.

PERRY, EDMUND. *The Gospel in Dispute.* Garden City, New York: Doubleday and Co., 1958.

RAINES, ROBERT A. *New Life in the Church.* New York: Harper and Bros., 1961.

RICKARDSON, ALAN. *A Theological Word Book of the Bible.* New York: The Macmillan Co., 1951.

ROBERTS, A. and DONALDSON, J. (eds.). *The Ante-Nicene Fathers.* New York: Charles Scribner's Sons, 1907.

ROBERTSON, A. T. *The Pharisees and Jesus.* New York: Charles Scribner's Sons, 1920.

ROBINSON, WILLIAM. *Completing the Reformation.* Lexington, Ky.: The College of the Bible, 1955.

ROWLEY, H. H. *The Biblical Doctrine of Election.* London: Lutterworth Press, 1950.

RUTENBER, CULBERT G. *The Reconciling Gospel.* Philadelphia: The Judson Press, 1961.

ST. AMANT, PENROSE. "Roman Catholic Church," *Encyclopedia of Southern Baptists.* Nashville: Broadman Press, 1958.

SCHURER, EMIL. *A History of the Jewish People in the Time of Jesus Christ.* New York: Charles Scribner's Sons, n.d.

SELWYN, E. G. *The First Epistle of St. Peter.* London: Macmillan & Co., Ltd., 1952.

SMART, JAMES D. *The Rebirth of Ministry.* Philadelphia: The Westminster Press, 1960.

—————. *The Teaching Ministry of the Church.* Philadelphia: The Westminster Press, 1954.

SMITH, H. SHELTON. *Changing Conceptions of Original Sin.* New York: Charles Scribner's Sons, 1955.

SOUTHARD, SAMUEL. *Pastoral Evangelism.* Nashville: Broadman Press, 1962.

SPIKE, ROBERT W. *In But Not of the World.* New York: Association Press, 1957.

STRONG, A. H. *Systematic Theology.* Philadelphia: The Judson Press, 1907.

TORBET, ROBERT G. *A History of the Baptists.* Philadelphia: The Judson Press, 1950.

TORRANCE, T. F. *Royal Priesthood.* London: Oliver and Boyd, 1955.

TRUEBLOOD, ELTON. *The Company of the Committed.* New York: Harper and Bros., 1961.

—————. *Your Other Vocation.* New York: Harper and Bros., 1952.

WAXMAN, MEYER. *A History of Jewish Literature.* New York: Bloch Publishing Co., 1930.

WILDS, ELMER HARRISON. *The Foundations of Modern Education.*
New York: Farrar and Rinehart, 1936.

WILLIAMS, DANIEL DAY. *God's Grace and Man's Hope.* New York:
Harper and Bros., 1949.

WINTER, GIBSON. *The Surburban Captivity of the Churches.* Garden
City, New York: Doubleday and Co., Inc., 1961.

WHITE, R. E. O. *The Biblical Doctrine of Initiation.* Grand Rapids:
Wm. B. Eerdmans Publishing Co., 1960.

——————. *Into the Same Image.* Nashville: Broadman Press,
1957.

WHYTE, WILLIAM H. JR. *The Organization Man.* New York: Simon
and Schuster, Inc., 1956.

Yearbook of American Churches, National Council of the Churches
of Christ in the U.S.A., 1961.

Index